swedish
INTERIORS

swedish INTERIORS

RHONDA ELEISH &
EDIE BERNHARD VAN BREEMS

Photographs by Jon E. Monson and L. Langdon Ergmann

Gibbs Smith, Publisher

TO ENRICH AND INSPIRE HUMANKIND

Salt Lake City | Charleston | Santa Fe | Santa Barbara

I dedicate this book to my parents, Cathy and G. Eleish, and my daughter, Kari.
—R.E.

A book for my two Northern Lights, Lars and Martin.
—E.B.v.B.

First Edition
11 10 09 08 07   5 4 3 2 1

Text © 2007 Rhonda Eleish and Edie Bernhard van Breems
Photographs © 2007 Jon E. Monson and L. Langdon Ergmann

Published by
Gibbs Smith, Publisher
P.O. Box 667
Layton, Utah 84041

Orders: 1.800.835.4993
www.gibbs-smith.com
www.evbantiques.com

Cover designed by Sheryl Dickert Smith
Interior designed by m:GraphicDesign / Maralee Oleson
Printed and bound in China

Library of Congress Cataloging-in-Publication Data

Eleish, Rhonda.
  Swedish interiors / Rhonda Eleish and Edie Bernhard van Breems ;
photographs by Jon E. Monson and L. Langdon Ergmann—1st ed.
    p. cm.
  ISBN-13: 978-1-4236-0024-4
  ISBN-10: 1-4236-0024-X
  1. Interior decoration—Swedish influences. 2. House furnishings—Sweden.
I. Van Breems, Edie Bernhard. II. Title.

TX311.E43 2007
747—dc22

2006031220

PAGE 2: During the mid-eighteenth century, trade with the Far East was made accessible thanks to the established Swedish East Indian Company based out of Göteborg, Sweden. As a result, the Swedish aristocracy and wealthy merchant class commissioned furniture that mimicked elements borrowed from the fashionable Far East. Unable to afford the expensive lacquer finishes of their Asian counterparts, the Swedes relied on faux paint finishes to achieve a similar result. Linda and Lindsay Kennedy's eighteenth-century, black-painted Rococo writing desk represents an ideal example from this period.

OPPOSITE: A view from the reception room into Libby Holsten's winter dining room reveals bare pickled floors, pale milk washed trim, and fanciful chinoiserie murals to set the stage for a Swedish eighteenth-century mood.

Rare Rococo Swedish side chairs in their original finish flank the breakfast-
room table. A Swedish Rococo tea table sits under a portrait.

contents

foreword
MIGUEL FLORES-VIANNA

My father specialized as an orthopedic surgeon at the Karolinska Institute in Stockholm. From an early age, I heard stories at home about the wonderful country of Sweden—of long summer days and endless winter snows. It was perhaps not a coincidence that I visited Sweden two months after Papa's death. I remember the first day in Stockholm walking around in a daze, looking for the faces that, I imagined, had known my father. Little did I know that his memories of that country would become my own as I got to know that wondrous land.

The world had changed a great deal by the time of my arrival in Sweden. My father's Sweden was quintessentially the 1960s, full of social exploration, of new boundaries and possibilities—Sweden was then at the forefront of all that. My world was the 1990s, and the Sweden that I came to know and love was very different.

My profession as a New York magazine editor had brought me to the country in search of beautiful architecture, inspiring interiors, and a very definitive sense of design. My various visits to Sweden, thereafter, and my meetings with members of the Swedish design communities, increasingly gave me a deep appreciation for how the citizens of that country view spaces that they inhabit in their daily lives—whether their home spaces are guided by principles of the eighteenth century or the twenty-first. Throughout that land, there is an appreciation for space, light, certain types of color, noble materials, and surroundings that I have not often seen in other countries. The Swedes are at ease with the world, and their homes are a microcosm of the world as they see it: elegant and simple—whether traditional or contemporary—always unpretentious, warm and well lived. These characteristics are well understood and admired by their American cousins. I always say, in fact, that our country speaks English, but in its love for equality and freedom, it is a Scandinavian nation at heart.

The houses in these pages are American homes that have tried to capture the essence of their Scandinavian counterparts. This is a first in American book publishing, and it is no surprise to me that my friends Edie van Breems and Rhonda Eleish have authored it. Their work as antiques dealers specializing in Swedish eighteenth- and nineteenth-century furnishings has made them not only experts in design, but has given them a deep understanding of how and why Sweden has influenced the American home. I hope you will enjoy these pages as much as I did, and if this is your first encounter with Swedish design, may this be the beginning of a long love affair!

Skål! ❀

OPPOSITE: The strong lines on an early-nineteenth-century, blue-painted Swedish chest of drawers are juxtaposed with the lines of the primary-colored wall sculpture by American artist Donald Judd.

foreword
ALBERT HADLEY

When one thinks of Swedish design and decoration, one conjures in one's mind and imagination visions of aristocratic and sophisticated examples that have been beautifully featured in such various publications as *Neoclassism in the North* by Håkan Groth, *The Swedish Room* by Lars and Ursula Sjöberg, *The Swedish House* by Lars Sjöberg, and other equally fine publications. The images that have been presented represent Swedish design in its full-blown splendor—a unique splendor of a given time and place. There is no denying the superb quality and cool allure afforded by such images—images that represent a total philosophy and a point of view of people whose lives are rich in historical investigation and interpretation. For the most part, it is architecture and design of august measure, and measure that causes one to return to a dream state without further pursuit of possibilities in the realm of personal expression.

Swedish Interiors opens wide the doors of possibilities for personal dreams and investigation. In this extraordinary book by Edie van Breems and Rhonda Eleish, one is enchanted, and yes, a bit surprised, by the multitude of examples put forth through means of photographic magic that show Swedish design in all its charm and beauty, very much "at home" in American houses.

In this ravishing volume, one visits vicariously a wide range of distinctive and personal houses where their owners have combined elements representative of their own personal taste; in each case, a taste that is diverse while at the same time expressing a strong and knowledgeable aesthetic.

Swedish Interiors comes full round: for instance, in an old log house where the interior walls are indeed the logs themselves, the furnishings are of appropriate earthiness and primitive quality. One is happily surprised to find ravishing examples of primitive Swedish furnishings and appointments performing with stage assurance alongside their American counterparts.

Another brilliant example is a house of more open plan employing soaring walls of multipaned glass—the spaces artfully punctuated by furnishings and objects of both Swedish and American design.

Edie van Breems and Rhonda Eleish offer the reader a great opportunity to witness these various and many properties where the inhabitants—obviously people with imagination and daring—share with enthusiasm and hospitality their superb examples of Swedish design in America. ❀

OPPOSITE: In the reception hall of the residence of the Swedish Consul General, New York, a set of five "Kassorskestolar" (cashier's chairs) designed by G. Asplund for Svenskt Tenn, circa 1929, are set dramatically under a painting of birch trees by acclaimed Swedish still-life artist Phillip von Schantz (1928–98).

preface

What is Swedish style? Generally in the United States, we have become very familiar with the Swedish Gustavian style, with its neutral tones and clean lines, as seen on the covers of most shelter magazines; however, the depth of Swedish design and color is much more expansive than just the white-hued images we have become accustomed to. As antiques dealers and designers specializing in eighteenth- and nineteenth-century Swedish antiques and interiors, we have long been aware of the diversity and beauty in both the soothing grays and whites of the Gustavian era, as well as the richness of the Swedish Baroque, Rococo, and Biedermeier periods. Most recently, Swedish modernism has also become a force in itself.

Swedish design is popular today, and its beauty lies in the confidence to mix both old and new. A stunning apartment in Stockholm will boast eighteenth- and nineteenth-century antiques, mostly family heirlooms, with recently acquired modern and contemporary art and furnishings. The desire to mix—whether furniture imported from abroad or antique versus modern—has been in the Swedish vocabulary since the sixteenth century.

Throughout the course of our business, we have been asked time and again by our clients, hungry for information, for resource information regarding Swedish interiors that is relatable to American homes. Given that America is a large and expansive country, finding resources that encompassed east, west, north, and south was not an easy task. This type of compiled resource just has not existed until now. Swedish interiors and lifestyle are becoming very popular in the United States, and we felt that there was a need in the market for a book that detailed American homes inspired by Swedish interiors. We kindly asked friends, clients, and colleagues across the United States to share their homes and spaces, and without hesitation, we found that they were just as passionate about sharing their love of Swedish style as we were.

Knowing how closely our cultures have crossed paths over the centuries, it is amazing how little is known about Sweden and Swedish decorative arts in the United States. It is our goal, with *Swedish Interiors*, to begin a dialogue that will excite and inspire those who read it, and show the diversity, depth, and mix-ability of Swedish design.

We hope that you enjoy *Swedish Interiors* and we thank everyone who opened their hearts and homes to us, and who shared in this incredible journey. ✦

OPPOSITE: The heart and soul of Sweden lies in the understated Swedish country folk antiques, or *allmoge*. To understand a country and its people, you really have to examine how the simple folk lived. In contrast to the wealthier merchant and noble classes, the farmers, mostly dairy and agricultural, lived a harsh life where survival of the family was the ultimate goal. The interior colors of their homes reflected what natural pigments were available to them, and handicrafts became a source of income during the cold winter months. The decorative arts flourished, and traditions sprang out of functional forms. For example, a simple mangling board used for ironing became a ceremonial symbol for marriage and union when carved by the fiancé of a young bride.

THE ORIGINS OF
swedish design

Swedish style mixes wonderfully with other vernacular styles; Swedish country furnishings look perfectly at ease in an early twentieth-century California bungalow, eighteenth-century Gustavian style revivifies a Rhode Island sea captain's home, and Swedish mid-century modernism adds pizzazz to a venerable Park Avenue mansion. In further examples, a Montana ranch weathers the elements in Swedish *stuga* style and Swedish high-country style warms a Connecticut gambrel roof colonial. Why does Swedish style mix so effortlessly with these various interiors? To understand this is to understand the country of Sweden itself and how its people have come to live and embrace their country's unique features and location in the world.

Sweden is a country of geographic extremes. The south is rich and fertile and the coastlines, with their great waterways and archipelagos, open up onto the riches of the Baltic and North Seas. Farther north lie great pine forests, giving way to a barren and arctic mountainous landscape marked by winters of great length and intense cold. Historically, Swedes needed to become one with the rhythms of the vast wilderness around them in order to survive. Self-sufficiency was a necessity and looking towards nature for inspiration, well-being, and connectedness became ingrained in the Swedish character. The environment played a vital role in the interiors of both the aristocrat and the farmer; however, it is in the homesteads, where life was much harsher, that the direct effects were more visible. The long, dark winter months contrasted so greatly to the Swedish summer's constant light. In order to maintain an interior balance throughout the year, Scandinavian style allowed for the maximum amount of light to enter their interiors, even in the darkest days of winter. As light was at a premium, crystal and reflective mirrors (though more commonly found in wealthier homes) were used to draw additional light from outside. Interiors were clean, painted with light and earth-toned colors, sparse (yet not cold), efficient, and very welcoming.

The decorative influences established by the Swedish royal court, beginning with the late sixteenth century, had a trickle-down effect on the rural homes of northern and southern Sweden. Most often, due to geographic isolation, decorative trends would take twenty or thirty years to become established in the more rural areas of the country. As a result, many wonderful examples of country furniture were created; rural artisans took forms found at court and re-created these items using secondary woods and paint surfaces to emulate the finer woods of the aristocracy. To truly grasp what Swedish style is, we have to look at what architectural and decorative trends influenced the Swedish court, and, also, how the rural Swedish farmers adapted those elements to their lifestyles, creating culturally what we relate to more today as Swedish design and lifestyle.

OPPOSITE: An elegant dining room is easily achieved when simplicity is the focus. The secret to Swedish style is keeping design pure and uncomplicated, allowing the beauty of the furniture and its environment to stand out.

Sweden's link to the outside world has always been the Baltic Sea, and Sweden's influence during the seventeenth century spread out from the Baltic well into areas of what is now Russia, Poland, Germany, and Estonia. Karl XII, Sweden's ill-fated warrior king, lost many of these territories and Sweden entered the eighteenth-century content to recede from a dominant position on the international stage. Trade with Holland, England, and Germany was strong during this time and a distinct Anglo-Dutch influence can be felt in the interiors of the Baroque period. Interest in the Far East became fashionable due to the accessibility of the growing import/export market established by the Swedish East India Company in Göteborg in 1731. Sweden's court and nobility were anxious to prove themselves to still be a cultured and thriving nation in spite of their remote regional location, and they eagerly adopted trends that were fashionable on the Continental scene.

Established in 2002 by Linda and Lindsay Kennedy, Chloe Decor specializes in original painted surfaces and fine patinas rather than provenance. Displayed here is a collection of Swedish tall-case clocks representing many different provinces of origin.

European aristocracy during the seventeenth and eighteenth centuries adopted some of the most sumptuous styles of decorative painting ever seen for their Baroque and Rococo interiors. Amazing *grisailles, trompe-l'oeil* moldings, marbleizing, gilding, and wood graining came out of Italy and France. The influence that French decorators and painters had on Sweden was considerable. Architects from Sweden would not only visit France for inspiration but would also make a point of acquiring the latest engravings for interior decoration such as Blondel's *Cours d'Architecture*, and the design folios of Jean-Charles Delafosse and Juste-François Boucher. Swedish crown architects and designers, notably Nicodemus Tessin the Elder, Tessin the Younger, Carl Hårleman, and Jean Eric Rehn, commissioned some of the finest French painters of the day to work on Swedish palaces and manor houses. These painters, in turn, apprenticed many Swedish painters under themselves. By the end of the eighteenth century, these Swedish decorative painters began to wander the countryside, bringing to the upper and middle classes the luxury of having their homes lavishly decorated, a status symbol previously only afforded to noblemen and aristocracy.

Trends on the Continent were towards using rare and exotic woods such as rosewood, mahogany, and burls, as well as marbles and porphyry, and decorative painters simulated these materials on walls and furniture. The Swedish adaptation of this type of faux finish ranges from the very sophisticated in the noble houses to the charmingly rustic and naïve in many of the country homes. Decorative painting, for all levels of society, was actually a very functional solution to Sweden's lack of certain resources. The country had a profusion of mighty evergreen pine forests, and rich and productive copper and iron mines, but very little in the way of other building materials. Lime—mixed in hues of marigold and reddish coral derived from local mining by-products such as cadmium, iron, and chrome-oxide—was painted onto mortar. In this manner, the Swedes were able to simulate French limestone blocks and bricks. Pine floors were also pickled with an application of limewash to imitate Italian carrera marble. Aside from replicating stone, all of this liming had the practical effect of allowing the underlying surfaces to breathe and acted as a fungicide and insecticide, preserving the wood

and mortar. Both urban and rural Swedish cabinetmakers beautifully adapted European examples of fine hardwood furniture in their native painted pine, creating simpler, elegant Swedish forms, thus saving the expense of imported exotic woods.

Itinerant painters usually had to mix their paints with what was locally available and—in Sweden's dairy- and flax-based culture—casein paints, along with egg tempera, colored by native mineral pigments, were cheap and easy to make. In fact, Swedish country furniture can often be identified by region simply by the paint palette used. Fine paneling and wallpapers were prohibitively expensive, delicate, and simply not available in the countryside so folk painters painted canvases to duplicate them. They used motifs and patterns less formal than the court painters and more inspired by nature and the surrounding countryside. The beloved floral garland intertwined with *trompe-l'oeil* moldings and the *kurbits* derived from the pumpkin plant (whose leaves and flowers transformed into an abstract ornamental pattern) come to mind as Continental decorative concepts that were absorbed and transformed into purely Swedish motifs.

Towards the middle of the eighteenth century, there was a return to all things classical. Unlike the Baroque interest in Greco-Roman style, the neoclassical movement that swept Europe was concerned with purity of form. The exciting discovery of the ruins of ancient Pompeii and Herculaneum in 1761 inspired new interest in classical designs. Sweden's young and cultured king, Gustav III, was a great proponent of this new classical style and journeyed himself to Italy to view firsthand the wondrous archeological discoveries. He brought back to Sweden all manner of classical antiquities and sculpture, intent on proving Sweden to be a cultured and sophisticated power, on par with France. The Gustavian style became synonymous with symmetry, fluted straight surfaces, and soft tones of gray and white, as well as thick garland and ribbon decorations and a continued vogue for Far Eastern wares.

Changing taste was not the only thing responsible for Swedes embracing this new Gustavian style. By the late eighteenth century, Sweden had passed many antiluxury laws, which ruled out the use of wood and metals for sheer ornament. The Gustavian style was simple, elegant, and easy to replicate; in its purest form it lasted until the 1830s, posthumously outlasting its own namesake by more than thirty years.

King Gustav III's war with Russia depleted the nation's coffers, leading to his assassination in 1792 and political unrest. In the period between King Gustav's assassination and the appointment of Crown Prince Karl XIV Johan in 1810, Sweden suffered a period of low moral and economic lethargy. In 1810, Jean-Baptiste Bernadotte, one of Napoleon's Marshals, was appointed to the Swedish throne. French by birth, Bernadotte introduced a fresh perspective to the Swedish court and soon after he was crowned Prince Karl XIV Johan of Sweden (and later, King Karl XIV Johan), Sweden began the slow recovery from the death of Gustav III and the economic effects of the Russian war. Court interiors, during the early nineteenth century, reflected the vigor and power of military campaigns, and thus Swedish Empire style was born. Swedish Empire style (more commonly known as Karl Johan style in Sweden) borrowed elements from the Empire movement, as well as incorporating the severeness of the French Directoire style. These styles were then adapted using lighter, indigenous woods, eventually maturing and becoming what we call Swedish Biedermeier in the mid-nineteenth century.

Sweden's transition from a poor agrarian-based society to a modern industrial nation was not an easy one. Rural life, towards the mid-nineteenth century, turned to misery due to famine and economic depression. Sweden's continued population growth was simply not being absorbed by the now-overcrowded industrial centers. Wages were low and there were overcrowded conditions. Land reform, famine, and blight hit the rural parts of the country; most notoriously the Bad Harvest of 1867–68, in which thousands starved to death and many subsisted on the infamous bark bread, in which ground bark had to be used to supplement flour. Times were hard and from 1850–1914 over one million Swedes emigrated, mostly to America.

The Swedish exodus to America had begun in 1841 with the first nineteenth-century Swedish settlement in New Upsala, Wisconsin.

Historically, Sweden was also an active participant in American expansion and independence in the early colonial period. Adventurous Swedes began to travel to the colonies in 1638 (just eighteen years after the *Mayflower*) and in 1655 a large Swedish settlement, Fort Christina, was established in Wilmington, Delaware. As the struggle for independence ensued, many Swedish colonists took up arms, joined the Continental army, and fought against the British. Just as importantly, Swedish settlers brought with them their cope style log building techniques, which were widely copied and helped to ensure safe settlement in the vast American wilderness. Now, during Sweden's darkest time, news came from across the Atlantic from established Swedes that America was a land of opportunity and a fresh start.

Large Swedish settlements were established in Iowa, Illinois, and Minnesota. Immigrant Swedes contributed mightily to the settling of the West. No strangers to harsh living conditions, rural Swedish farmers brought their old-world farming techniques to America and thrived. The impact of the migration to America by Swedish immigrants was substantial. Just one example shows that by the turn of the twentieth century 12,000,000 acres of farmland were owned by Swedes and 150,000 first and second generation Swedes were recorded as living in the city of Chicago. Interestingly enough, the city of Chicago had the largest concentration of Swedes in one location, with the exception of the city of Stockholm. By 1920, one in every five Swedes lived in America.

As Sweden recovered emotionally and economically at the end of the nineteenth century, revival styles dominated the decorative arts. Thanks to publications like England's *The Studio*, Art Nouveau (or *Jugendstil*, as it was called in Sweden) became popular. The Arts & Crafts movement, with its emphasis on looking back into England's heritage for inspiration, also spoke to Swedes at a time of burgeoning nationalism and a strong desire to save their own traditional heritage. With tremendous foresight, the *Nordiska museet* was founded in 1873 to preserve Swedish peasant culture, the *Handarbetets vänner* was founded in 1874 and worked for a revival of textile art by bringing back old Swedish techniques and patterns, and *Föreningen svensk hemslöjd*

(Swedish Handicraft Society) was established in 1899 to study old crafts and provide new work for craftsmen. Skansen, the world's first open-air museum, was opened in 1891 to preserve and celebrate Sweden's architectural past.

A new appreciation for traditional designs, with an emphasis on integrity of craftsmanship, was a reaction against shoddily made mass-produced goods and—more tellingly—a yearning for and romanticization of Sweden's past. The most famous proponents of this aesthetic were artists Carl and Karin Larsson, whose old frame house in Sundborn, in the Swedish province of Dalarna, was immortalized in Larssons' books "Ett Hem"(*A Home*) and "Mot Solsidan" (*On the Sunny Side*). Using widely diverse furnishings from different periods, repainted in bold colors that integrate into the rest of the house, the Larsson home is one of the first and best examples of a what we now know as "Swedish Modern" interior. For Karin and Carl it was all in the mix: functional, fun, and personalized. It is no wonder, then, that the Larssons' country home, with its cheery, bright, light-suffused interiors and happy family of occupants, became one of the most beloved, best-known and iconic examples of Swedish design to reach the world.

Perhaps because the Swedish climate nurtured a life centered around the hearth, interest in the home and its furnishings has always been important to the Swedes. In the twentieth century, in particular, Swedish designers became concerned with what critic Gregor Paulsson advocated as "more beautiful things for everyday use." By the 1930s, Erik Wettergren, secretary of the Swedish Society of Industrial Designers, had ensured that important Swedish artists, such as Wilhelm Kåge and Edward Hald, were working in conjunction with Swedish porcelain and glass companies so that fine design could be on the tables of everyone. Designers like Josef Frank started breaking away from strict functionalism and began using organic shapes and bright, surprising color combinations in furniture and textiles. By the 1950s and 1960s, Sweden's concept of enlightened product development was well established and Sweden became internationally known for overall design excellence. Today we continue to look towards Sweden for practical yet beautiful examples of how to live.

Given the rich history of design throughout the centuries, specifically decorative arts and interiors, it is no surprise that the popularity of Swedish design continues to inspire and influence. In our journey to create a well-balanced book, we were pleasantly surprised by the locations we found, and how examples from the different periods in Sweden were evident. Creatively styled, the homes photographed in *Swedish Interiors* represent elements of the Baroque, Rococo, Gustavian, Biedermeier, Carl Larsson, and Modern styles that have lovingly been married with regional American settings and interiors.

There is a long tradition in America of immigrants bringing the customs, as well as the decorative and architectural arts of their homelands, to American shores. The Swedes were not unlike any other immigrant group in this regard and in many ways this tradition continues on to the present day. Much of this book focuses on contemporary Swedes who have adopted America as their country and have melded the very best aspects of Swedish design and sensibility into their American homes. Americans, too, have discovered and been inspired by the full range of Swedish design with a basis in functionality, naturalness, and cleanliness of line that is very similar to their own national aesthetic. ❁

gustavian grace

"There are books which take rank in your life with parents and lovers and passionate experiences," wrote poet and philosopher Ralph Waldo Emerson. This was certainly the case when designer Libby Holsten stumbled upon some books on Swedish interiors of the Gustavian period. "My aesthetic up to that point had been Italian Renaissance and French Provincial . . . and then I saw these haunting photos of Sweden. This was so different in that there weren't rugs or window treatments. The wonderful colors, the naïveté of the wall paintings, the crystal sconces and chandeliers—it was all wonderful."

OPPOSITE: Elegant tones of cream, beige, and white give the large Pool House living room an ethereal quality. A statue of frolicking, carved, wooden cherubs rests on the table.

THIS PAGE: Libby's reception room windows are curtained in muslin. In Sweden, muslin curtains were used to filter the glaring sun of endless midsummer days. An early-nineteenth-century horse is placed next to a painted commode.

Inspired, Libby proceeded to amass an extensive collection of Swedish eighteenth-century furniture, with which she furnished her homes in Newport and Boston. Despite the beauty of these two homes, a 1795 colonial in a coastal town in Rhode Island would ultimately prove to be the perfect place to fully exercise her passion for Swedish interiors. Although the house had been all but abandoned and was in a state of extreme decay, Libby, with her discerning eye, instantly knew that the rooms would adapt easily to Swedish design. "The square rooms, the enfilades, the roofline, the light from the water—it was all there. Meanwhile, my husband, George, and the realtor were just standing there shaking their heads."

Undeterred and immune to protests that this crumbling manse might prove to be her Waterloo, Libby threw herself into the restoration project with gusto. And what of the Swedish design books? "They were my bible! My artist friend Odette Holty and I painted side by side referencing these incredible historic Swedish manor homes for ideas." Libby, although unaware of it, was working in a manner very similar to Swedish interior designers of the eighteenth century, who would bring back folios of the latest architecture and design trends from the Continent. These folios, mostly from France, were then used as points of reference (as Libby used her books) from which designers such as Carl Hårleman and Thomas Rehn would work with their painters and cabinetmakers, creating the uniquely pared-down, elegant Swedish interior finishes we are familiar with today. Libby and Odette implemented many types of Swedish faux finishing techniques throughout the house. A whimsical chinoiserie faux wallpaper is painted in the entrance hall and stairwell in subtle shades of taupe and brown. In the salon one finds a medallion head of a nobleman in grisaille, and faux bookshelves line the adjoining hallway leading to the powder room.

After nine months, the restoration was complete and in a style that even Gustav III, Sweden's culturally progressive king (for whom the Gustavian style is named) would be proud. The original dark, cold palette had been replaced with ivories, grays, and blues. French doors had been installed, where possible, to let in more light,

and rotted flooring had been replaced with pickled oak and pine. Faux finishes were used liberally throughout the house. Libby brought in rooms full of antique Swedish furniture and, like any sophisticated Swede from the Enlightenment, freely mixed the Swedish furniture from her collection with the French. Admiring Libby's collection of musical instruments, books, and rare antiquities, you wish that Gustav III, who shared similar passions, would stop by, if only to view the portrait of himself as a young prince that hangs in Libby's reception room.

When asked about the enduring appeal of Swedish design, Libby exclaims, "I don't understand how something so simple can be so interesting . . . other rooms I have designed have been so exciting . . . but then, the excitement level pales with time. These rooms . . . I think it gets better. The Swedish furniture excites me more every day." ❁

OPPOSITE: Libby's entrance hall is painted in chinoiserie. Faux finishing was used extensively in Swedish eighteenth-century interiors. (Before the eighteenth century, textiles were used almost exclusively to provide color and warmth to walls.) As the East India Company opened trade to the East, significant quantities of porcelain and lacquered furniture began to be imported to England and France. The exotic nature of these imports and tales from travelers fueled a taste for oriental decoration in Sweden. "Chinoiseries," oriental scenes based on paintings and tapestries, became very popular among the noble classes of Sweden. The most famous example of this is the Chinese pavilion at Drottningholm with interiors designed by Jean Eric Rehn.

THIS PAGE: A Swedish Rococo bench makes a sculptured statement in Libby's Pool House. The fluid curving of the Rococo style was quickly adopted in Sweden, characterized by its rocaille, or shell, carvings and amorphous slat backs. In fact, wonderful examples of Swedish Rococo can be found that date past the 1750s, a time after which the style had already gone out of favor on the Continent.

THIS PAGE, LEFT: The influence of the China trade was very prevalent during the eighteenth century. The painted black-and-gilt pine clock in the winter dining room is a Swedish version of the black-lacquer-and-ormolu clocks found on the Continent during the period.

THIS PAGE, RIGHT: Libby's rare blue delftware collection is nestled in an alcove built into the front stairwell.

OPPOSITE: Soothing shades of cream and gray set a restful tone in the winter dining room, while white-and-gold porcelain on the mantelpiece adds sparkle and a neoclassical motif. An early-nineteenth-century four-tier crystal sconce from Sweden hangs above a Swedish 1820s bed. Brown and mauve pillows in antique toile add a touch of warmth.

The afternoon light silhouettes a nineteenth-century harp in the Salon. Swedish formal pieces mix seamlessly with French furniture as they are most often derived from that vernacular. The antique cello looks perfectly at home next to the French cream-painted biblioteque and the gilt Louis XVI settee.

Understated Swedish grandeur can be found in Libby's Salon. A fine example of a 1790 Swedish settee makes an inviting seating area, while a white-painted Swedish secretary and a Stockholm clock with works by Jean Wessman add height and balance to the room. Gustavian side chairs line the room. A 1780s painted Swedish tea table holds the last of the summer lilies.

THIS PAGE: Paneling was used extensively in eighteenth-century decoration. Lacking the material to create fully paneled rooms, such as their European contemporaries, Swedish architects and designers during the period cleverly used faux finishing techniques to splendid effect. Libby takes a cue from the salle at Skogaholm Manor, now part of the Skansen Museum in Stockholm, using simple gilded half-round moldings and hand-sketched field panel detailing to create a sumptuous but bright atmosphere.

OPPOSITE, LEFT: A Swedish clock dating from the 1780s.

OPPOSITE, TOP, RIGHT: A French grisaille hangs on the wall surrounded by ribbon swag delicately painted by Libby and Odette.

OPPOSITE, BOTTOM, RIGHT: A 1780s Swedish carved gilt clock.

OPPOSITE: Libby did her kitchen all in cream. A set of Swedish Gustavian chairs gather round an early-nineteenth-century pine trestle table. The ample built-in shelving houses Libby's china collection.

THIS PAGE, TOP: White-and-gray faux marble walls and pickled hardwood floors keep things light in the bathroom.

THIS PAGE, BOTTOM: The bathroom doubles as an ethereal retreat complete with a nineteenth-century Swedish desk. In typical Swedish manner, muslin sheets serve as curtains, creating beautifully diffused light. A Swedish nineteenth-century clock sits in the corner.

THIS PAGE, LEFT: The simple beauty of a nineteenth-century Swedish pine trestle table is singular. It traditionally served as the centerpiece of a Swedish farmer's home around which meals and indoor work took place. During banquets the table would be covered in handspun linen. A portion of a Swedish wall canvas is framed and hung over a table, reinforcing its folk origins.

THIS PAGE, RIGHT: A whitewashed Bornholm clock and a Gustavian chair add serenity to the guest bedroom.

OPPOSITE: A small Swedish hanging cupboard adds to the back stairwell.

new sundborn

THE WISCONSIN RANCH OF LORAN NORDGREN

Loran Nordgren, on a trip to Sweden, found himself at his family's region of origin, Dalarna, the folk art–infused rolling land north of Stockholm. It was there that he came upon the door of Carl and Karin Larsson's legendary home in Sundborn. Called Lilla Hyttnäs, the home became famous for Larsson's painted depictions of its interiors where he recorded the simple pleasures of his family life.

OPPOSITE: Lou Heiser pushed Loran to paint the house in more aristocratic (by Swedish standards) ochre, in order to stand out from the ubiquitous red barns of the Wisconsin landscape.

THIS PAGE: The welcoming entryway to the Loran Nordgren house has a covered porch with benches. It is based on the entrance to a farmhouse in Northern Hälsningland.

At the turn of the twentieth century, when Larsson's books on Lilla Hyttnäs were released, there was a movement in Sweden to go back to the old ways, very similar to the Arts & Crafts Movement in England. Karin and Carl Larsson were at the forefront of this movement, reacting against industrialization. Their home was a revolutionary design statement at the time. They furnished the rooms with unfashionable folk decor that they painted in daring, bold colors. In fact, every surface of the house is brightly painted and the overall effect is sunny and light. The Larsson home was at once an inspiration and an epiphany to Loran—here was the type of retreat he envisioned for his family.

Loran Nordgren had purchased a tract of Wisconsin land in the Coon Valley region in the 1970s. There, he and his family came on vacations to camp, fish, and hunt on the land, but Nordgren had not yet built a homestead. He came back from Sweden excited and ready to break ground. He wanted to build not just a home but a family compound based on the Swedish courtyard model. Nordgren called into service his longtime associate, designer and architect Lou Heiser, to draw up plans of the house and oversee its building. When asked about the Nordgren house Heiser says, "The totality of the whole project took over my whole life . . . it really was a once in a lifetime project—all consuming—as you can imagine."

A sight was chosen and the foundations for the house were built into a hillside overlooking a valley on the property. Wide planks were cut from trees found in the surrounding forest and woodcarvers and artisans were contacted to realize Loran's vision of a handcrafted home. The home was to consist of four buildings loosely built around Sweden's ancient courtyard model: the house, a guesthouse, a garage with pavilion overlooking the pond, and a traditional storehouse shed.

The finished result is a playful and warm homage to the spirit of country Swedish style. As in the Larsson home, every surface is painted and personalized. What appears to be a deceptively simple use of cheery colors throughout the house is, in actuality, a sophisticated, twenty-four-color, tonal tour de force only art directors and designers of Nordgren and Heiser's caliber could pull off. Detailing is everywhere, from hand-carved eagles to hand-cut scalloped moldings. A delightful set of three built-in

OPPOSITE: Reproduced Gripsholm chairs and ottomans, upholstered in homespun red-check cotton, make for an inviting family room. The focal point of the room is the authentic tile *kakelugn*, or wood-burning ceramic stove, that Loren imported from Sweden. Invented by Johan Cronstedt and Fabian Wrede in 1767, the *kakelugn* was much more efficient than open hearths and is a mainstay of Swedish interiors from the Gustavian period.

THIS PAGE: The names of Loran's children—Erik, Tracy, Loran II, Lauren, Carl, and Robert—are painted in yellow lettering around the perimeter of the family room.

beds awaits guests in the cottage, balconies and nooks and crannies abound, and a gazebo surprisingly sits on the roof of a garage ready for smorgasbords and mid-summer gatherings.

New Sundborn, as the house is lovingly referred to, is not only a testament to Lou Heiser as a designer and architect but also a testament to his and Loran's vision and whimsy. "I had the advantage of knowing Loran's personality and that helped a great deal and [I] was blessed by the many wonderful local artisans."

It is no surprise to anyone who meets Loran Nordgren that he would feel a kinship to Larsson's vision of home. Like Larsson, Loran has an optimism bred from a tough childhood converted into hardworking ideals. Having built up and sold his Chicago advertising firm, Loran has come back to his beloved Wisconsin retreat to live full-time. Here he raises prize alpaca and indulges a love of flying his antique planes. He is legendary among the Amish children in this rural farming community for dropping bags of candy from the skies. Here is a man not just copying Larsson's home pastiche, but really creating his own way of living. Ideals, curiosity, and a strong love of his family are most important to Loran, as evidenced by the names of his children and grandchildren painted on the walls alongside inspirational sayings. Painted by artist Sandra J. Russell on one of the many beautiful walls of New Sundborn is this: Loran's Rule: "The first thing is to last."

Loran Nordgren has succeeded in building a home that will surely last in the lives and hearts of his family for generations to come. ❦

OPPOSITE, TOP: A Bornholm-style clock, based on a traditional clock form originating from Bornholm Island in the Baltic Sea, stands at attention by the hallway. Swedish rag rugs are found throughout the house.

OPPOSITE, BOTTOM: This wall painting hangs over a doorway in the family room, with Carl Larsson's advice from the wall of his home, directing us to "Love One Another Children, For Love Is All."

THIS PAGE: A Dalarna bed settee, dated 1825, is painted Falun red with blue detailing.

OPPOSITE: The hearth was the center of the *stuga*—the traditional Swedish country cottage. Here the hearth and stove are brought out into the heart of the kitchen to warm the family when they gather around the eighteenth-century trestle table.

THIS PAGE, TOP: Saunas are an integral part of Swedish lifestyle. Detoxing and refreshing the body by sauna is part of almost every Swedes' fitness routine. Loran's sauna has an etched-glass mural of sauna accoutrements—hot stones, ladles, and birch branches.

THIS PAGE, BOTTOM: Artist Sandra Russell based this wall painting on a Swedish wall canvas called *Lord of the Servants* from the town of Rättvik, signed "DAS."

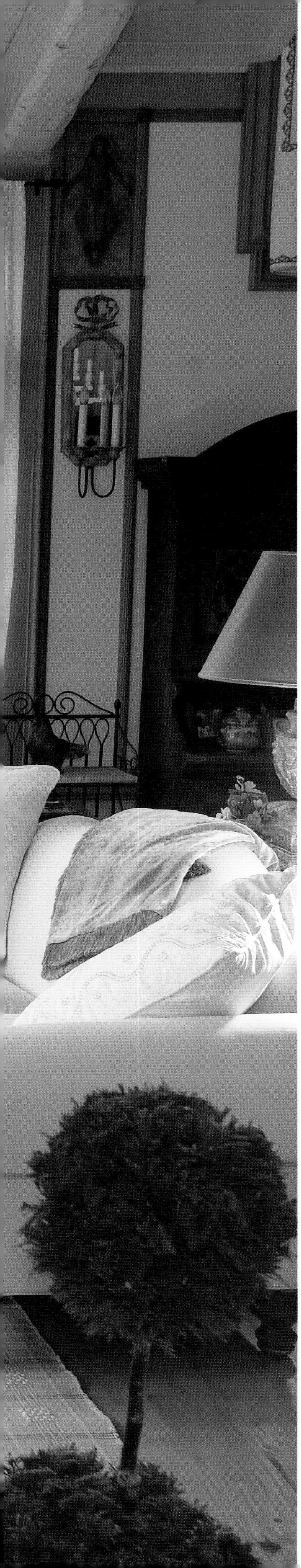

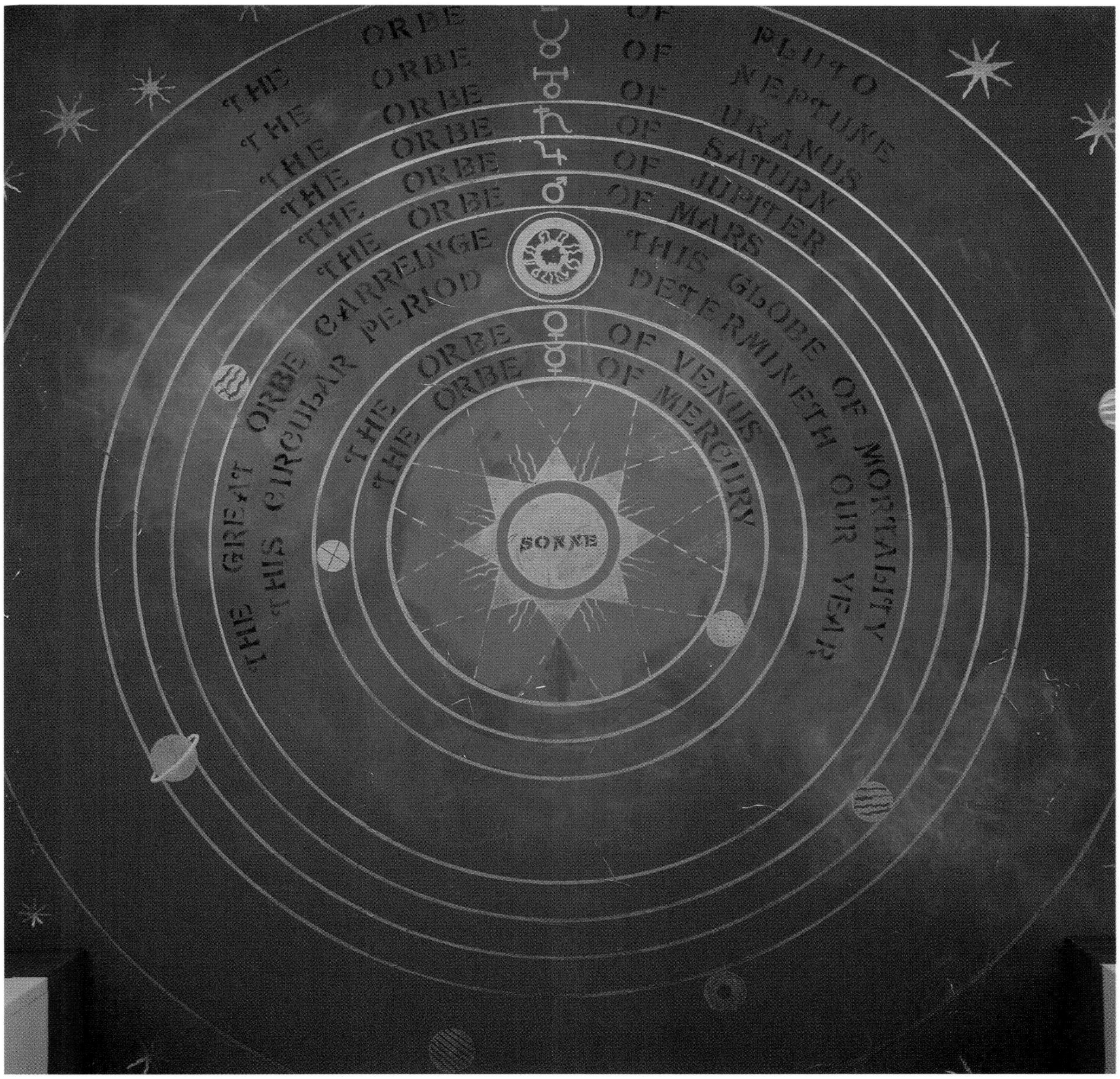
THE ORBE OF NEPTUNE
THE ORBE OF URANUS
THE ORBE OF SATURN
THE ORBE OF JUPITER
THE ORBE OF MARS
THE GREAT ORBE CARREINGE THIS GLOBE OF MORTALITY
THIS CIRCULAR PERIOD DETERMINETH OUR YEAR
THE ORBE OF VENUS
THIS ORBE OF MERCURY
SONNE

OPPOSITE: The colors of the living room are soft and formal. Transom windows were built to replicate the leaded windows in Carl Larsson's studio. The border around the top of the ceiling is based on the stenciling in Karin Larsson's bedroom.

THIS PAGE: The celestial ceiling in the nook of the window seat is based on a 1576 drawing of the celestial orbs.

OPPOSITE: Loran's bed is an exact replica of Carl Larsson's bed at Lilla Hyttnäs.

THIS PAGE, TOP: This built-in cupboard bed with scalloped proscenium is a child's dream come true. There are three such built-in beds on the second floor of the cottage. Traditionally this style of bed was built into an alcove of the *stuga* and was heavily curtained to keep in warmth.

THIS PAGE, BOTTOM: Loran built a guest *stuga*, protected by whimsical carved dragons, with built-in beds for all of the family. Dragons were popular figures in medieval Swedish carving motifs, as seen on opposite ends of the roof.

OPPOSITE, TOP: The barn is painted Falun red, the traditional red paint of Sweden derived from the copper oxide of the great copper mine of Falun. Grasses thrive on the charming sod roof.

OPPOSITE, BOTTOM: Some of Loran's prized alpacas. The alpaca herd at New Sundborn numbers about thirty at any given time. Among them is El Bello, the champion son of legendary alpaca stud Hemingway.

THIS PAGE: Loran uses the storehouse built on the steep sloping hill of the central courtyard for farm lectures, gatherings, and parties. The sod roof is typical of Scandinavia.

california bungalow
HOME OF LINDA AND LINDSAY KENNEDY

I magine the perfect summer day, where the sun is abundant and you're as close to paradise as you can get. Linda and Lindsay's Los Angeles bungalow, a surprising escape from city life, yet still in the city, is just that. Built in 1923 as part of a Mormon community development, the bungalow was restored in 2001 by architectural interior designer Nancy Fishelson. Known for restoring antique homes and then going on to the next project, Nancy had already restored the home when the Kennedys approached her to see if she was interested in selling the bungalow to them. Luckily, she was, and they placed their current house on the market. By spring 2003, the bungalow was theirs.

OPPOSITE: The whitewashed walls act as a perfect foil for Linda's design sensibility. Attracted to paint finishes rather than provenance, Linda and Lindsay specialize in finding original paint surfaces that evoke a charmed response. The interior white backdrop and the vintage homespun linen, slip-covered furniture allow for the beautiful patina of the antiques to stand out while anchored down by the dark floors.

THIS PAGE: Restored by Architectural Interior Designer Nancy Fishelson, the Kennedy's L.A. bungalow was a perfect match for their lifestyle and business, Chloe Decor.

The bungalow was in move-in condition, and was perfect for the couple since they had just started Chloe Decor, their Swedish antiques business in L.A. The Kennedys had been on the search for a home that would perfectly complement the Swedish antiques they had been collecting for the business, and when they stumbled upon the bungalow they knew they had found the right location.

The only part of the property that still needed attention was the garden. Over the next six months, the Kennedys slowly installed the plantings around the bungalow, completing the final steps of restoration. By taking their time, Linda and Lindsay were able to settle into their new home and let their new space determine what plantings would be best.

The charm and whimsy of the garden are a reflection of Linda's Swedish design style. The main entrance of the property is set back from the house, gated by eighteenth-century Swedish doors. Once past the doors, you feel like you have entered a secret garden, hidden from the hustle and bustle of L.A. city life. Continue towards the bungalow, and you encounter citrus trees, hydrangea, mock orange,

ABOVE: Attracted to the clean, elegant lines of Swedish antiques, Dealer/Designer Linda Kennedy incorporates modern soft seating with a late-eighteenth-century Swedish tall case clock, two demilune tables back to back, and pewter chargers.

OPPOSITE: The use of simple window treatments allows for the sun to stream into the house during daylight hours.

plum, and peach trees, an English rose garden, and a very large old avocado tree that Linda and Lindsay have lovingly nurtured. Discreetly placed amid the greenery, chaise lounges offer guests the perfect location simply to enjoy a beautiful day.

When asked what inspires Linda and Lindsay, the answer is both simplicity and design influences from European shelter magazines. When they opened Chloe Decor in 2002, their business was primarily wholesale. Linda, a Swedish native, now spends a majority of her time focusing on her thriving interior design business; and Lindsay, a California native, spends his time on the retail side of the business. He is also a restaurateur. Their partnership and talent are the key factors to their success.

When it comes time for a buying trip, Linda brings their son Christopher for a visit with family in Sweden, and Lindsay joins them a few weeks later to tie up all the shipping details. It seems now that even young Christopher has the design bug. His favorite pastime is to push furniture around the house, mimicking what Mom and Dad do. If all early indicators prove right, Christopher will be a great asset in the business, following in the footsteps of his talented parents. ❁

OPPOSITE: Function and form were the key components of Swedish design in the eighteenth and nineteenth centuries. Gustavian in form, this late-eighteenth-century clock secretary served many purposes. Working under the premise that space was limited, a very clever cabinetmaker crafted a secretary that was not only functional but also visually stunning. Rather than have two pieces of furniture in the room taking up precious space, why not merge them?

THIS PAGE, TOP: Because interior space was not abundant in the eighteenth and nineteenth centuries, Swedish tables, for example, were designed to function within the space constraints as well as have the ability to expand during festive events.

THIS PAGE, BOTTOM: A Swedish tall case clock was commonly found in homes in Sweden beginning in the mid-eighteenth century and throughout the nineteenth century. The origin of the Swedish Mora clock began in and around the Mora Municipality in Dalarna County in a small town called Östnor during in the late eighteenth century. The clock works were crafted by farmers, the first reported to be Krång Anders Andersson (1727–99), who needed to find additional income during the winter months. The prolific iron mines of nearby Sala made iron ore very attainable and affordable for the farmers to work with, hence the clockwork industry grew. This communal cottage industry started as a small moneymaking venture by a few farmers, and by the end of the nineteenth century, an estimated 50,000 clockwork motors were produced. In most instances, the clock cases were built separately from the clockworks, and as a result, clock cases varied by region in form and color. A clock case crafted in the south varied greatly from a case crafted in the north. Forms evolved in the eighteenth century from a straight case to a curvier "female" form in the nineteenth century. This was due primarily to the advances in technology that enabled the cabinetmaker to produce a case with more curves. Today Swedish tall case clocks are commonly called "Mora Clocks," however, only clockworks and cases produced in the Mora Municipality can accurately bear the name of Mora. Not all Swedish tall case clocks are Mora clocks.

THIS PAGE: A nineteenth-century American bed with crisp linens, antique Swedish furnishings, and rag rug runners work perfectly together, creating a charmed bedroom for Christopher.

OPPOSITE, TOP: Lindsay, a professionally trained chef, finds their kitchen a joy to create in. With tonal white-on-white balanced out by potted herbs, the Kennedy's kitchen is a reflection of elegant simplicity.

OPPOSITE, BOTTOM, LEFT: The Kennedys' collection of Swedish antiques is not limited to large pieces. Linda has started to collect antique Swedish wooden farm bowls as well as Swedish ironstone. These accessories lend an enormous amount of charm to the kitchen when creatively displayed together.

OPPOSITE, BOTTOM, RIGHT: Choosing not to electrify the candlelit chandelier above the dining room table, Linda and Lindsay re-create eighteenth-century Sweden during dinnertime.

OPPOSITE, TOP: Due to the groundbreaking work of the famous Swedish botanist Carl Linnaeus, Sweden became the center for the study of natural sciences in the mid-1700s. First to document and classify many of the earth's plantings in *Systema naturae* (1735) and *Species Plantarum* (1753), Linnaeus brought to life the study of botany, which was still in its infancy prior to his work. *System naturae* and *Species Plantarum*, still used today as points of reference, had a great influence nationally. Interest in botany became fashionable, and the love of nature became a passion, as it still is to this day. It is no surprise then that Linda, a native of Sweden, fell in love with the property at first glance.

OPPOSITE, BOTTOM: Linda and Lindsay's enchanted garden path leads to their Swedish bungalow.

THIS PAGE: Scattered in the garden are various pause points created to enjoy outdoor dining and living.

TOP: One of the treasures displayed on the property is a nineteenth-century Swedish sleigh.

BOTTOM: A nineteenth-century Swedish farm trough is the perfect container for a display of late summer pumpkins.

TOP: The Kennedy's secret garden and bungalow lie beyond a pair of nineteenth-century Swedish doors.

BOTTOM: Initially started as a wholesale business, Linda and Lindsay opened the doors of Chloe Decor to the public due to an overwhelming response from their clients.

ten chimneys

HOME OF AMERICAN THEATER'S ALFRED LUNT AND LYNN FONTANNE

For a better part of the twentieth century, Alfred Lunt and Lynn Fontanne were toasted on either side of the Atlantic as the greatest acting team in the history of the English-speaking theater. By all accounts they were each witty, intelligent, charming, and passionately dedicated to their craft. The theater was their life. At their country home, Ten Chimneys, in Genesee Depot, Wisconsin, they created a laboratory and an idyllic retreat. It was a place where they could write, rehearse, and relax away from the scrutinizing eye of Broadway and the West End.

OPPOSITE: Green-shuttered Ten Chimneys, as viewed from the side, has traditional Swedish board and batten siding. Alfred installed the eight-sided star window.

THIS PAGE: Wall murals by set designer Claggett Wilson have lords and ladies hospitably greeting Alfred and Lynn's guests in the front hallway with food and drink. Painting on walls in nobles' houses was prevalent in Sweden during the 1760s with a particular fondness for French and chinoiserie themes. The paintings by Wilson are similar in feel to the Rococo Swedish painter Johan Pasch. The Rococo sconces and black-and-white tile flooring are the height of 1930s chic.

OPPOSITE: A rare eighteenth-century Swedish *kakel-ugn* stands at the end of the front hallway. A *trompe-l'oeil* proscenium with drapery frames the stove. Kakelugns can be tricky to install properly and usually an expert from Sweden needs to be sent in when reconstructing an authentic one.

THIS PAGE, TOP: Alfred and Lynn loved to rehearse for their latest play in the "flirtation room" because of its many doors. Note the Swedish tall case clock over-painted and embellished into a gilt confection, complete with grisaille French chickens and pastoral scene. The rooster on the top of the clock is made of brass.

THIS PAGE, BOTTOM: From the "flirtation room" you have a clear view of the bedroom hallway and stair-well, complete with Claggett Wilson's portrait of Gustav III. The wall treatment is découpage that Alfred and Lynn cut out and pasted there.

Luminous stars and theatrical personalities, such as Noël Coward, the Oliviers, Alexander Woollcott, Helen Hayes, Charlie Chaplin, and Katharine Hepburn all made the sojourn out to Wisconsin to be a part of this site of artistic inspiration, education, and collaboration. Carol Channing is famously quoted as saying, "Ten Chimneys is to performers what the Vatican is to Catholics. The Lunts are where we all spring from."

About thirty miles west of Milwaukee—mythic places are always a bit hard to pin down—Genesee Depot is nestled into the southwestern Wisconsin kettle moraine. Down the road from the train station, through a gate at the end of a country lane, you enter the private world of the Lunts. Alfred was of Swedish heritage and spent many joyous summers as a young man at a Swedish colony in Finland with his mother and stepfather. He purchased the land to Genesee Depot in 1913 and building began on the main house in 1914. There was a chicken coop on the property, and Alfred converted it into a cottage his mother would eventually live in after he married Lynn.

Extremely proud of his Swedish roots and inspired by his time in Finland, he built the cottage to look like a Swedish country house replete with covered entry and red-and-white trim. Within, he decorated the living room all in *allmoge*, the rustic, folk furnishings of Sweden. The feeling on entering the home is that you have just walked into a very wealthy peasant house with artful nineteenth-century Swedish textiles on display. Rather than hang the textiles on the ceiling, as would have been done traditionally, the Lunts made them into curtains. Wooden racks are built into the walls to display a collection of pewter plates. Pewter and decorative ceramic dishes were considered too fine for daily use in Sweden but were displayed in country homes to demonstrate wealth.

OPPOSITE: Alfred and Lynn had Claggett Wilson paint biblical scenes on the walls and ceiling of the great drawing room derived from paintings in Swedish manor houses and castles of the 1740s to 1780s. The paintings by Wilson are done in soft shades of apricot, pale yellow, and sea foam greens and blues.

THIS PAGE: A depiction of Jacob's Ladder is the focal point of the wall in the drawing room.

Alfred also collected early-twentieth-century replicas of *kurbits*, the traditional wall paintings of the Dalarna region of Northern Sweden. Based on biblical motifs, *kurbits* were paintings showing biblical figures and stories transposed into a vernacular Swedish setting. The marriage at Cana—a popular subject—was, for example, painted with the biblical figures in stylish Swedish dress of the early 1800s, and the architecture depicted was usually that of a nearby church or parish. The word *kurbits* comes from the pumpkin or cucumber leaf used to shade Jacob in the Bible. Swedish artists took the form of this plant and painted it into wonderful abstract patterns that are a hallmark of the style. Alfred clearly loved this style. When he did not have enough wall paintings to finish covering the walls of the cottage he painted them himself. It is supposed that Lynn posed for some of the figures.

In the main house the Swedish influence is expressed in a more formal context. Alfred convinced Claggett Wilson, set designer and friend, to pack up his paintbrushes and come out from New York to help put the finishing touches on Ten Chimneys. Entering the front hallway, guests are greeted by Wilson's wall murals of squires and maids dressed in eighteenth-century finery offering up drinks and delicacies in a restoration-style garden. Murals of this sort with life-size figures were part of a long tradition in seventeenth- and eighteenth-century European aristocratic castles and manors. Several wonderful examples can be found in Sweden, most notably in Tessin Palace and Skokloster Castle.

At the end of the hall is a very rare late-1770s Swedish ceramic stove. Wilson painted an alcove with draped curtains around it to emphasize the *kakelugn*'s importance. Inspired by Swedish biblical wall paintings, such as the *kurbits* in the cottage, Alfred and Lynn chose to use them again, now as a jumping-off point for the extensive murals and ceiling paintings in the large drawing room. Wilson painted biblical scenes such as Jacob's Ladder using a light formal color palette of soft pinks, apricots, sea foam blues, and palest greens. The figures are painted in the modernist style of the 1930s and '40s and share the walls with beautifully rendered animals. Wilson's most charming nod to Sweden is found in a stairwell off the drawing room. There a portrait of Gustav III as a young king in all his finery looks out from beyond a gilt frame festooned with garlands.

For more than sixty years, Alfred and Lynn lived, entertained, and acted on the stage they built for themselves at Ten Chimneys. It was quite a run, enjoyed by all who came throughout the years. After their deaths, the Lunts' elderly family stayed on for a while in the Swedish cottage, though eventually succumbed to the rigors and expense of carrying on such a large estate. Ten Chimneys, run down and in peril of being sold to developers, was saved by the single-minded vision of one man. Joe Garton, a Wisconsin businessman and self-proclaimed theater enthusiast, miraculously learned of the sale of the property moments before it was lost. (In that lies another tale that attests to the magic and spirits at work at Ten Chimneys.) Today Ten Chimneys is listed on the National Register of Historic Places and is tirelessly run by the Ten Chimneys Foundation for all to enjoy. The dream and preeminent home of American theater continues. ❈

Alfred, a gourmet cook, would indulge his love of all things culinary in the spacious kitchen. He reveled in growing his own vegetables and berries and kept a creamery on the property. The red-checked curtain and charming scallop-edged wood valance lend the kitchen a Swedish air.

OPPOSITE: The cottage was known affectionately as "the Hen House" because it had once been the chicken coop and later was where Alfred's mother stayed. Painted red with crisp white trim, the cottage is the very vision of the Swedish countryside with the addition of some stylish 1930s-style red-and-white-striped awnings.

THIS PAGE, TOP: The kitchen in the cottage has theatrical borders painted on the walls as if to emphasize the stage-set quality of a Swedish *stuga* transposed to twentieth-century Wisconsin. A seventeenth-century Swedish hanging cupboard sits on a rare red-painted Baroque Swedish double trestle table. The lettering on the door is Alfred's grocery list in Swedish. The word *fisk* is painted in red . . . speculation on this abounds. Is it Alfred's red herring?

THIS PAGE, BOTTOM: The corner stove has a charming faux backsplash painted in black.

THIS PAGE, TOP: A traditional nineteenth-century wood-and-wire chandelier hangs over the breakfast table in the kitchen. Cushions add comfort to antique Swedish pine farm chairs. The stencil border around the kitchen was painted by Alfred, who left all of the pencil marks from the outlines, as is done on stage scenery.

THIS PAGE, BOTTOM: An eighteenth-century Swedish gate leg table sits in front of a bed decoratively painted by a Swedish-American artisan from the early part of the twentieth century. A beautifully made bed, resplendent with linens, was a sign of prestige in peasant homes.

OPPOSITE: Light streams through the living room windows of the cottage, which are softly curtained by Swedish textiles. All manner of built-in cabinetry was used in *stugas*. Typically, a long built-in bench was installed to provide seating and storage along the wall facing the kitchen table. Early nineteenth-century iron candlesticks flank a wooden bowl on the table. This kind of candlestick derives from medieval Swedish smith work.

THIS PAGE, TOP: The wall of the cottage living room is papered with turn-of-the-century wall paintings in the style of Sunnerbo, Sweden. Around 1875 paper became widely available and instead of painting on canvas the Sunnerbo artisans were able to produce decorative hangings in mass. These appear to have been bought by Alfred on his travels. There were not enough hangings to finish the room so Alfred painted the rest himself.

THIS PAGE, BOTTOM: The hearth was the heartbeat of the *stuga* home, providing necessary warmth in the harsh Swedish climate. In the cottage's library, Alfred had a fireplace built in the traditional Swedish manner of the nineteenth century—built into a corner and sticking out at a diagonal into the room. Stylized *kurbits* patterns adorn the ceiling.

OPPOSITE: A grand metal chandelier ringed with bells hangs from the vaulted ceiling of the timber-framed studio. Plate racks line the walls as would be traditional in a *stuga*. A rare pair of Norwegian barrel chairs sits by the window. The pillows adorning the furniture are made of Swedish textiles.

OPPOSITE: Claggett Wilson designed this pool house, and the tower actually conceals a pump that carries water up to the cupola for showers. A group of nineteenth-century Swedish farm chairs, painted white and red, cluster around a table for alfresco dining.

THIS PAGE, TOP: The mermaid crowning the cupola was a gift from Cecil Beaton, hence the name "Mermaid Pavilion."

THIS PAGE, BOTTOM: A flower box cascades with summer flowers at the studio.

sweden in the tropics

LARS BOLANDER AND NADINE KALACHNIKOFF'S
PALM BEACH HIDEAWAY

ou have but to ascend a narrow staircase on palm-lined Worth Avenue to arrive at the gate of Lars Bolander and Nadine Kalachnikoff's hidden jewel of a home. Palms and hanging tropical orchids greet you as you enter onto a rooftop courtyard garden, which is the central passageway between two apartments that the couple have combined into a stylish spread. A Balinese-inspired thatched pavilion with an altar and umbrellas in the courtyard suggest that a tropical theme shall be found throughout and in no way prepares the visitor for what waits inside . . . the home of a Swedish eighteenth-century ex-patriot nobleman perfectly transported to this tropical paradise.

OPPOSITE: The white-paneled walls and sisal rugs of the living room instantly put you at ease, despite the grandeur of the furnishings. A gray Swedish tea table sits under a Swedish transitional Rococo clock. The settee is done in traditional Swedish red ticking, lending a sense of informality to the room.

THIS PAGE: The main wall of the living room displays treasures from an extensive art collection. A French grisaille of an angel floats above a collection of plinths.

THIS PAGE: Vaulted ceilings give a sense of soaring space
and lightness to the main living room. Bergéres are covered
in linen and create inviting seating around any bibliophile's
dream—a coffee table groaning with books.

Internationally renowned designer Lars Bolander is a master of contrast, effortlessly mixing styles and periods. Swedish period furniture, modern pieces, and hip objects picked up from around the globe are hallmarks of the three Lars Bolander stores (Miami, Manhattan, and Palm Beach). For their own intimate retreat in Palm Beach, Lars and Nadine wanted "an amusing place." This is not a hard task for these two, whose magpie eyes span centuries, juxtaposing times, finds, and cultures.

What waits inside their home is a collection of Swedish and French eighteenth-century antiques mixed with custom-designed furniture, all set off by a cool Swedish color scheme. The home's white-paneled walls, sea grass rugs, and open beams all serve as the perfect backdrop for a wonderful art collection. "Nadine and I have been very blessed in that art has always been central to our lives," says Lars. Their collection includes many eighteenth- and nineteenth-century portraits, sculptures, contemporary works of art, and antiquities; the sophistication of their collection is in the edit.

Contemporary works by Spanish and Italian artists mingle with Swedish court paintings. Lars and Nadine place authentic seventeenth-century bronzes next to their nineteenth-century counterparts. Similarly, nineteenth-century copies of still lifes take pride of place next to rare originals. The overall effect is that of being in the home of collectors who love beauty for beauty's sake.

Lars and Nadine found the apartments in this early twentieth-century Addison Mizner building nine years ago and since then have transformed the interiors with all manner of wall treatments, trompe-l'oeil, and floor painting done around classical themes. The feeling is that of being inside a

THIS PAGE: A Swedish pine demilune console table holds a collection of Italian busts and bronzes. The floor is painted to simulate marble tile, a historical technique found throughout Swedish manor houses and castles.

manor house whose owners have brought back all
sorts of treasures from their global travels. How
did it all come about?

"Inspiration is just something that you have,
and then, once you have that there is nothing
stopping you. Oh, and guts . . . yes, you must have
guts!" says Lars laughingly. "Really, I just love
changes and construction. I am constantly
changing this place." In reference to the Swedish
influence in his work Lars says, "It is amazing.
The palette has stayed with me. It does make you
happier to see these reflections." ❋

OPPOSITE: A Dutch girl in a Baroque frame surveys the dining room. A large bookcase by Nicky
Haslam grounds the far wall and through the doorway one can see the silhouette of a Swedish
tall case clock. The tone becomes softer in the dining room where the palette is sand and gray.
The painted architectural feature over the doorway is almost identical to the one found in
Tessin Palace in Stockholm.

THIS PAGE: A fire bucket filled with flowers on a burlap-covered occasional table tones down
the formality of the room. The mixing of humble, natural materials with the formal is a hallmark
of Swedish design.

OPPOSITE, TOP, LEFT: Under the canopy of the French mushroom are Russian candlesticks, silver shells, and shrimp, as well as Nadine's signature table setting—parsley filled silver goblets.

OPPOSITE, TOP, RIGHT: An eighteenth-century English portrait of a gentleman hangs over a Swedish settee.

OPPOSITE, BOTTOM, LEFT: One of a pair of rare Venetian busts of Blackamoors, circa 1780. Venice was an important seaport and throughout the centuries many Moorish rulers vied for control of the city. Images of the Moor, such as these busts, were particularly ubiquitous in Venice.

OPPOSITE, BOTTOM, RIGHT: A bust of Lars sits on the sideboard in the studio. Nadine says, "I just don't recognize him without his glasses."

THIS PAGE: The library is done in soothing butter-cream yellow. On the wall hangs one of two treasures, engravings of Gustav III and Queen Sophia Magdalena in their original carved and gilt frames.

OPPOSITE: A giant wooden mushroom from Paris is an imposing presence in the dining room. It complements the gray-and-cream diamond patterned floor.

THIS PAGE, TOP: Inspired by trips to Indonesia, Lars and Nadine designed the thatched cottage, a luxurious gathering place and cool retreat from the Floridian sun. Thatchers from South Africa were hosted to install the grass roof, and the roof's survival through numerous hurricanes is a testament to their talents.

THIS PAGE, BOTTOM: An Indonesian altar holds jade-and-crimson offering bowls and wooden Chinese figurines.

northern grandeur

RESIDENCE OF THE CONSUL GENERAL OF SWEDEN, NEW YORK

For over sixty years, on the corner of Park Avenue and Sixty-Fourth Street, a little piece of Sweden has been thriving in New York City under the watchful eye of The Consulate General of Sweden.

In 1946, the Swedish government purchased the building, along with the adjacent townhouses, and today it is used as the primary residence of The Consul General of Sweden. It is an Italian neo-renaissance palazzo, designed and erected between 1910 and 1911 for the merchant Jonathan Bulkley by one of New York's most fashionable architects of the time, James Gamble Rogers.

OPPOSITE: Guests are greeted in the grand nineteenth-century entranceway by a bold red carpet by contemporary Swedish designers Gunilla Lundborg and Bodil Karlsson for Kasthall, setting the stage for the dramatic contrasts of old and new to be found throughout the residence. Madeleine Hatz's painting *Blue Vault* can be seen through the doorway to the dining room.

THIS PAGE: Named after Karl XIV Johan, who ruled Sweden from 1818–44, the Karl Johan style is Sweden's parallel to the Empire style. Here, coffee is served in the sunny Karl XIV Johan salon. The portrait of the king himself is on loan from the National Museum of Fine Arts in Stockholm. The carpet by Ingegard Thorhamn gives the room an unexpectedly modern twist.

THIS PAGE, TOP: A Larson chandelier is the central focus of the dining room.

THIS PAGE, BOTTOM: Swedish hospitality reigns in the light-drenched dining room. The official Three Crown plates were commissioned from Sweden's venerable china manufacturer Rörstrand.

OPPOSITE: Furnished in decor by Josef Frank for Svenskt Tenn, the dining room is all modern elegance. Hide rugs were used historically in Sweden to provide warmth and were commonly used as throws on beds and in carriages. Here a hide is laid playfully on the black-and-white tile floor, stylishly referencing Sweden's roots. Simple muslin is hung around the perimeter of the room, providing softness while still allowing light to filter through.

The limestone walls, central arched doorway, pediment windows, and slate roof are all done in such a way as to give the building a delicacy and refinement that is found in many of its Swedish and Northern European counterparts done in the palazzo style of the period.

In 1981, the building was designated a landmark by the New York City Landmarks Preservation Commission, and the Swedish government began an extensive restoration under the surveillance of architect Lennart Jansson. What stands today is an elegant building, Nordic in air, with a feeling of joyous openness—a jewel nestled amongst the neighboring sky rises.

The residence of the Consul General of Sweden is very much a living building in that it is constantly evolving. Each Consul General and their family bring with them their own personal furnishings and style, adding their own individual stamp to the building. Although individual styles may come and go, what remains a constant throughout the building is the furnishings of Josef Frank for Svenskt Tenn. Svenskt Tenn design is, in fact, found in all of the Swedish embassies around the world because it is considered to represent the best of Swedish modern design. Its designs have become a large part of the Swedish heritage, mixing fantastically with contemporary pieces.

Founded in Stockholm in 1924 by Estrid Ericson and Nils Fougstedt, Svenskt Tenn sold striking modern designs in pewter and then expanded into furniture and textile design. Austrian designer Josef Frank joined the company in 1934 and his thirty-three-year design partnership with Estrid Ericson has become the stuff of legend. Rejecting minimalism in favor of organic, lavishly functional designs, Frank and Ericson created the Svenskt Tenn look. They freely adapted designs and colors from different cultures and periods, deftly using Frank's vibrant color schemes and graceful lines to unify the elements. The spacious dining room and library both have many fine examples of Svenskt Tenn textiles and furnishings.

Contemporary furniture, artwork, and textiles by prominent

Swedish designers and artists are also to be found throughout the residence. Contrasting the contemporary and modern against the architectural backdrop of subdued belle époque grandeur creates a tension and excitement. It is a technique that is used extensively in Sweden and can be especially experienced within the larger cities.

The broad mission of the Consulate General of Sweden is to promote Swedish culture and interests in the United States. To this end, the decor of the residence is a wonderful reflection and celebration of current and past Swedish art and design. A little corner of Sweden right in the middle of Manhattan is sure to inspire all who enter its doorway.

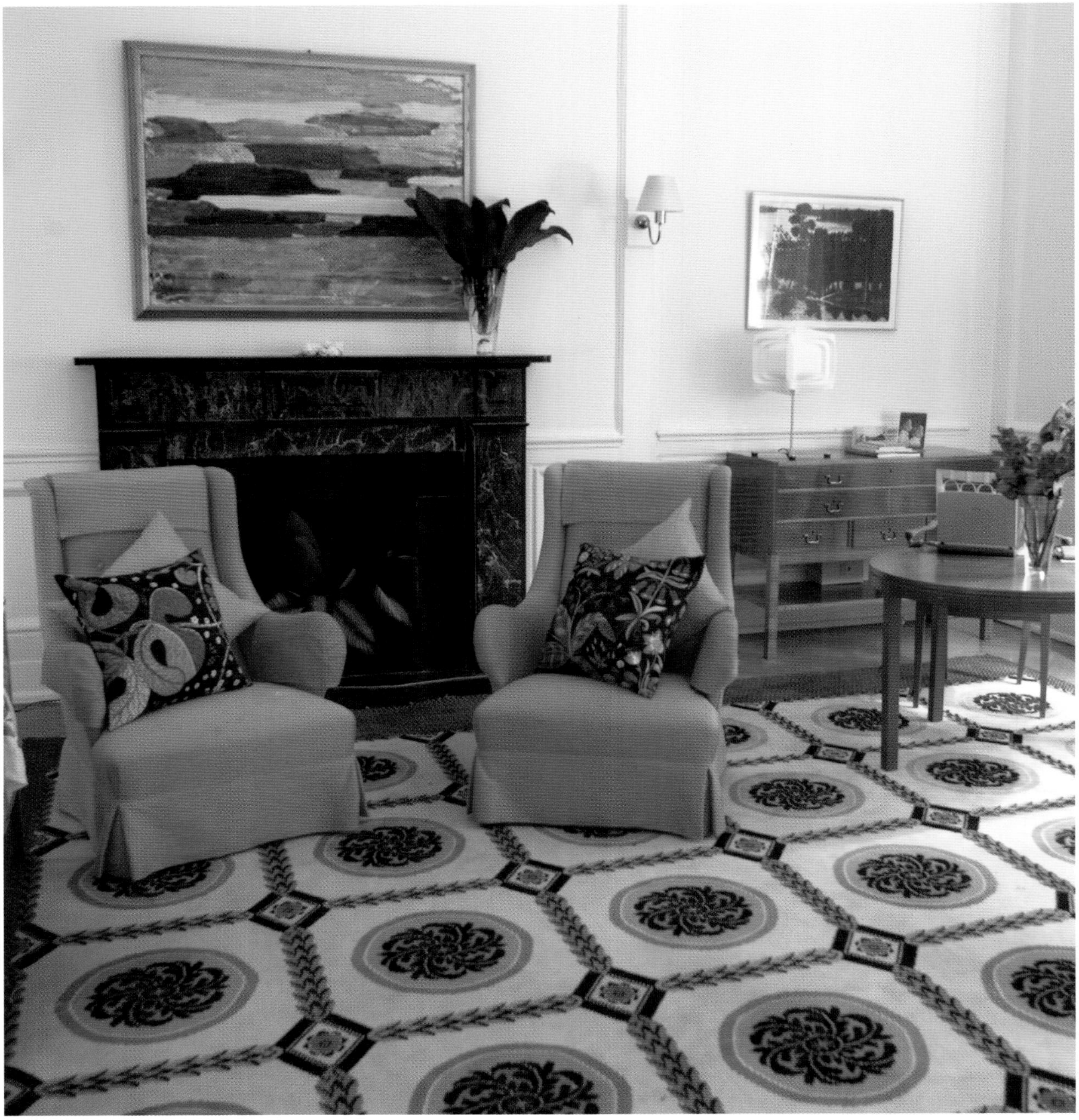

THIS PAGE: In the master bedroom, Torsten Bergmark's *Grå utpost* hangs over the mantel. The Malmsten chairs for Svenskt Tenn are upholstered in cheery, bright pink. A carpet specially woven after an example in the Royal Palace of Sweden ties it all together.

OPPOSITE: The ornate mirrored archways of the reception hall are echoed in the subtle circular pattern of the gray carpet designed by Åsa Lagerström for Kasthall. The contemporary sofa set is by Anna Kraitz. A sculpture, *Spirit of Transportation*, by legendary Swedish sculptor Carl Milles (1875–1955) sits on the mantel.

THIS PAGE: A reading table in the corner of the library sits on a Josef Frank carpet. The chairs were originally designed for the *Riksdag* (Swedish Parliament). A portrait of Greta Garbo by Carsten Reglid enigmatically surveys the room.

OPPOSITE: Colorful Svenskt Tenn sofas flank the library's imposing fireplace. Glass fruit by Swedish artist Gunnel Sahlin rests in a bowl next to a "myrten" teapot by Signe Persson-Melin for Svenskt Tenn. Above the fireplace hangs the "Triton Panel," a replica of the high-relief panel from above the door of the admiral's cabin in the Swedish seventeenth-century warship *Wasa*.

the swedish guesthouse
INTERIOR DESIGNER DIANA BEATTIE'S MONTANA HOMESTEAD

The Swedish immigrant homes—dating from mid-nineteenth century to the early twentieth century—scattered around the United States take their roots from the rural farmhouses found all through the Swedish countryside. As luck would have it, Diana Beattie, of Diana Beattie Interiors, discovered an authentic Swedish timber homestead northwest of Bozeman under the Bridger Mountains, not far from her Montana homestead. She lovingly restored it on her property, incorporating elements from its Swedish roots and cleverly mixing elements of its new environment in the American West.

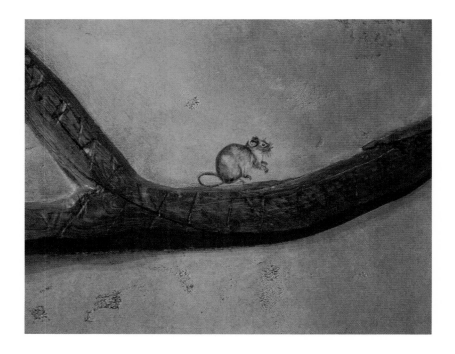

OPPOSITE: Combining both Swedish design elements and traditional western style, Diana wanted to pay homage to the lineage of the building while fusing it with a spirit of the West. Yellow ochre walls, a Swedish trestle table and painted corner cabinet from the North of Sweden, and the lack of window treatments represent key components of a beautiful Swedish country interior. Diana was inspired by the folk art of Dalarna, Sweden, which served to underscore her love of painted furniture and then expanded to walls, stairs, and light fixtures.

THIS PAGE: What country cottage does not have a resident critter or two? Diana's whimsical approach to that question is found on the staircase wall leading to the upstairs master bedroom.

Once the Swedish cabin was purchased, Diana set about researching traditional Swedish interiors and studying the designs of the famous painter Carl Larsson. During this period, she began to collect antique folk furnishings for the interior and commissioned David Laitinen (an artisan carpenter of Norwegian heritage) to build authentic Swedish folk furniture with its decorative details. Diana then asked Jennifer Bessen, a *trompe l'oeil* artist and glazer, to create authentic Swedish finishes and faux painting throughout the cabin. According to Diana, "With the help of architect Candance Tillotson Miller, and those artistic Montana builders, Yellowstone Traditions, the house was 'restacked' and interiors finished within nine months, making it ready for guests to float back to another century in this Swedish re-creation."

The original homestead had two stories. Diana added a lower floor, which housed another bedroom, a large bathroom, and a laundry/utility room. Diana also replaced an old pre-Franklin stove with two corner fireplaces, built with the rock tailings from the old gold-mining operation on the Beattie property. She set floor-to-ceiling stone fireplace surrounds into the corners of the main floor's living area and the lower level's bedroom. On the top floor, the master bedroom was updated with the addition of a bathroom, and a working kitchen was added to a corner of the main floor.

The Swedish log cabin was originally built in the late 1800s by the Forswall brothers of Sweden. According to David Laitinen, the artistic carpenter who originally discovered the building, "At least two brothers spent some months building the log cabin using logs that were manageable in size for two men to stack. They beautifully performed the shaping in the tradition of their family and their homeland region using tools they had made. The house logs are skillfully cut with hand saws, squared, coped, and dovetailed with axes, and turned to smoothness on the outside surfaces by skillful working of an adze."

The home's interior was all dressed with traditional Swedish folk painting; doors were combed with yellow paint, patterned in wavy, parallel designs. Denim was the selected gasket material (rather than mortar) for the seal between the length of the logs. The walls

The need for the warmth and light of the sun to fully filter into a space, enhanced by bold yet warm colors, is typical for a Swedish country home's interior. Diana has achieved this by using a warm color on her walls as well as leaving her windows open and bare to capture the maximum amount of light.

The mines of Falun, Sweden—considered to be some of the finest in all of Europe—enabled both the aristocrat and commoner to have copper vessels to serve decorative and functional purposes. Diana, inspired by the beauty of Swedish copper, applied copper surfaces within her cottage kitchen, highlighted by nineteenth-century Swedish culinary copper. Using aged copper for the counters, sink, and even to mask the refrigerator, Diana perfectly matched the patina found on her antique Swedish copper pots and pans.

THIS PAGE: One has to look more than once to realize that the clock at the top of the stair isn't really a clock.

OPPOSITE: The warmth of Swedish ochre combined with this American four-poster bed creates a rustic partnership that is both inviting and comfortable.

had been framed with 2 x 4s laid flat; these were notched into the logs on their irregular inside to make them plumb for superbly flat walls on the inside and were then paneled. Outside, the logs were hewn so smooth that 2 x 4s were easily nailed flat to the logs before adding a layer of 4-inch cedar lap siding, which minimized heat loss and protected the house logs from the elements. David reports that "the cabin was lived in for decades before the family stopped improving the home, and eventually built a bigger home. Fueled by the love of family, the time-consuming creative hard work was done in tribute to their loved ones as well as to the natural, indigenous material which had recently become available from a relatively new item to the area: a circular sawmill. The house was likely painted as was common throughout history in Swedish folk tradition, by its owners in the winter while farmwork allowed some time for work at home."

Diana Beattie, known as the interior designer who loves collecting old buildings, has saved and restored many wonderful log and hewn barns and historic homesteads for her clients. She creates whimsical and very detailed homesteads that are not only beautiful structurally, but also artfully restored to the very last detail. Diana's talent naturally comes to her, and so when you visit one of the homes that she has designed, you are amazed that she has addressed and ingeniously presented detail beyond your imagination. ❀

TOP: Inspired by Swedish box beds, Diana commissioned David Laitinen to craft and Jennifer Bessen to paint these wonderful examples. They double as couches and are used as extra beds when friends and family come to visit.

MIDDLE: Above the box beds, Jennifer Bessen painted historically accurate examples of Swedish folk art wall coverings that were inspired by the wall coverings from the northern Swedish province of Dalarna. Dalarna, a wealthy region due to the abundant copper and iron mines, had a larger concentration of wealthier farmers as well as the industrial wealth generated from the mines than most provinces in Sweden. Because of the availability of employers, traveling folk painters found employment, and a richness of work was established in that region. Though based primarily on biblical subjects, the folk paintings, *"Kurbits,"* later documented weddings, deaths, births, and good harvests. The above garlands were commonly painted to welcome the arrival of spring and to remove the cold, long, and dark winters they had just experienced.

BOTTOM: Decoratively painting simple architectural elements, such as an interior door, adds dimension and interest to a surface that would otherwise be overlooked. Historically, Swedish decorative painters enjoyed creating visual impacts on interior surfaces to give the illusion of more space. *Trompe-l'oeil* artist Jennifer Bessen achieved this by decoratively painting this interior door with floral panels above and the biblical scene of Adam and Eve in the Garden of Eden on the bottom panels.

LEFT: Diana's love of nature and the clever use of elements found on the homestead property add whimsy to the Swedish guest cottage entrance by using willow branches and a "pinecone man" on the front door. Crafted by David Laitinen, the double-facing benches on the front porch are also very traditional examples of Swedish creativity. Further examples of David's creative artistry are found throughout the property.

RIGHT: Love, marriage, and family are traditionally celebrated in Swedish folk paintings. Borrowing from that theme, decorative painter Jennifer Bessen lovingly re-creates a seventeenth-century marriage scene on the inside of the front door, welcoming today's romantics staying at the Swedish guest cottage.

OPPOSITE, TOP: Diana was delighted to hear about the discovery of an original Swedish immigrant's homestead, though in sad repair. Known for her love of historic buildings, Diana jumped at the opportunity of restoring the building to its original beauty and purchased the homestead from a farmer.

OPPOSITE, BOTTOM: Though a homestead with all the modern comforts, Diana has remained adamant about maintaining the historic integrity of this old mining property. It is easy to feel transported back to the nineteenth century when you are on its premises.

THIS PAGE, LEFT: A small shed lies behind the Swedish guest cottage with additional bunk beds. Traditionally, Swedish homesteads were comprised of multiple dwellings around a courtyard, leaving the main house at the head of the courtyard. The family lived in the main house, and the workers and animals lived in the surrounding buildings. Single-handedly built by artisan carpenter David Laitinen, the Garden House was built as a cabin for the grandchildren.

THIS PAGE, RIGHT: Notice the clever use of a bent branch as a door handle to the garden shed. Restoration glass was used to add age to the windows and door. The monochromatic tones of gray are replicated in the 100-year-old hewn timbers, on the rock tailings used in its foundation, and on its weathered door.

romance on the bayou

JOHN RABALAIS' NEW ORLEANS HOME

✻

Everyone just loves Swedish furniture, so I always carry a few pieces because they are so appealing," says Gerrie Bremermann, a Louisiana interior designer. "I'll never forget when John came into the shop and fell for some Swedish furniture." The gentleman she speaks of is native New Orleanean John Rabalais. John fell hard for Swedish. A discerning and energetic professional, he made a point to learn all he could and then began to collect Swedish antiques, particularly Gustavian, in his spare time. By the time he teamed up with Gerrie again to decorate his new home on the Bogue Falaya River, "he had a whole garage full of Swedish furniture," says Gerrie. "I don't know where he got it all!"

OPPOSITE: Gerrie painted the brick walls white in the solarium and filled it with Swedish furniture painted white and pale shades of gray and blue. On the wall hangs a painting by Jamie Meeks. The delicate legs of the nineteenth-century Swedish table appear fragile when put against the Louisiana brick flooring. Two carved wooden cherubs hover over a distressed eighteenth-century Swedish commode.

THIS PAGE: Approached through the garden, a cherubic fountain greets John's guests. The wonderful weathered bricks are native to Louisiana soil.

John Rabalais is not the first to fall under the spell of Swedish Gustavian furniture. Named after Sweden's King Gustav III, the style is characterized by clean, elegant lines and neoclassical detailing. It is a style that evolved from the furniture of the French court of Louis XVI and was brought back to Sweden by Gustav III and his architects and designers. The trend was to move away from the excesses of the Rococo period and redecorate using elegant, classical forms. Swedish furniture of the period was generally made of pine and then painted over. The patina acquired over many years on these Gustavian period pieces gives them a quality that is particularly beautiful. Gustavian-style furniture is so popular in Sweden and well loved internationally that it is still being manufactured today.

When John bought his house (designed by Louisiana architect Al Jones) and approached Gerrie to do the decorating, she knew exactly what to do. Ironically, she had decorated the house two other times for different clients. "I guess you could say, three times the charm," giggles Gerrie. The homes of Al Jones are known to incorporate historical aspects of Louisiana's architectural past, and the Rabalais house is no different. Wide pine planks are found throughout the home, and nineteenth-century salvaged Louisiana beams and bricks are used to give depth and texture to the relatively new—by New Orleans's standards—structure. Because of the heavy French influence on Louisiana's history and the great impact of the French on Swedish design, it seemed very natural to meld the French and

Swedish together in this most southern of homes.

Drawn to the waters around him, John knew that he wanted to live with colors that reminded him of the ocean and sky. "Pale and changing blue, grays in all shades" are what John says appeal to him. Due to his demanding schedule, he also needed a place that was not only elegant but totally relaxing and comfortable to come home to, with well-appointed guest rooms for friends and visiting relatives. To this end, Gerrie began to help John decorate the spacious rooms in cool confections of sea foam greens and blues mixed with soft Gustavian colors. She also created numerous seating areas around the house that are so inviting no one ever wants to leave them. The sofas are well cushioned, and large down-filled French bergères are used wherever possible. Gustavian furniture is not usually thought of as comfortable, but Gerrie and John chose a pair of eighteenth-century Swedish barrel chairs. It is a surprise and a delight for anyone who sits in them to discover that they are ergonomically designed. Even the strict Gustavian settee in the living room is made to sink into, with a thicker-than-usual checked cushion and masses of Becky Vizard pillows made from eighteenth-century textiles. The fabrics Gerrie used are sumptuous, such as Fortuny velvets, but when chosen in soft tones and mixed with the Swedish furniture the effect is rich yet not imposing.

John has remarked that his favorite part of the project was finishing it. As the banks of the river rose up to his back porch during the days of Hurricane Katrina, you can imagine thoughts running through his head that all of his hard work and vision might be lost. Miraculously, the waters stopped at his door and his Swedish-French vision remains a place of calm light amongst the sweet, long leaf pine and Spanish moss. ❧

OPPOSITE: This French-inspired home was built by Louisiana architect Al Jones using native brick. The home sits majestically along the tree-and-moss-lined banks of the lazy Bogue Falaya River.

THIS PAGE: In the hallway, a rare Rococo Swedish gaming table with soaring legs is flanked by two eighteenth-century, delicately hoofed Swedish barrel-style side chairs. A Swedish tall case clock stands sentinel at the doorway.

THIS PAGE, TOP: Swedish furniture holds its own in a very formal French room. The strong lines and gray tones of the Gustavian settee and chairs appear very clean and stand out beautifully against the more ornamented French fire screen, trumeau, and coffee table.

THIS PAGE, BOTTOM: A palette of cool grays and blues creates an ethereal mood in the grand living room.

OPPOSITE: A traditional pine Gustavian sideboard in black and white provides ample storage space in the den.

OPPOSITE: Gustavian painted chairs gather round a French walnut wine-tasting table in the solarium. By the doorway sits a Swedish tall case clock with especially fine leaf-and-berry carvings.

THIS PAGE, LEFT: A delicately carved wooden angel from John's collection acts as a guardian in the front hallway.

THIS PAGE, RIGHT: This Swedish tall case clock dates from 1790 to 1810. Here is a fine example of how formal neo-classical motifs merged with native Swedish designs. Note how the dentil molding and leaf carvings add a touch of Gustavian formality to the traditional bridal-figure clock body.

THIS PAGE: A mood of soothing calm is set in the master bedroom by a George Marks painting. A pair of Swedish painted side tables flank the bed.

OPPOSITE: Light streams in through the French doors leading onto the terrace from the bedroom. A Swedish tabouret upholstered in striped silk sits before a distressed, gray, painted French commode.

country elegance

HOME OF FACE STOCKHOLM'S MARTINA ARFWIDSON AND
RESTAURATEUR DAVID WEISS

❖

aised in Sweden, Martina has a strong connection with her mother, Gun Nowak; the relationship was not
only one of mother and daughter but also of friend and spiritual partner. In 1980, Gun founded Face
Stockholm, a cosmetic line, which was an immediate success. She soon realized that she would need help
running the business, and she turned to Martina, who was in New York following a singing career. Martina says,
"When I started working with Mom, Face Stockholm became about something else besides selling lipstick.

OPPOSITE: Sunlight fills the living room, and you instantly feel comfortable and relaxed. Martina's approach to interiors is "Every house is different and evokes a different feeling for me . . . the light and space itself dictates what needs to happen." The use of white slipcovers anchored by the darker wood furniture allows the sun to be absorbed into the space and yet be grounded.

THIS PAGE: A nineteenth-century Swedish painted tilt-top candle stand not only serves a functional purpose next to its contemporary companion, but also becomes a piece of sculptural art as opposed to just another antique table in a room filled with furniture.

I could see the link that this business shared with music—bringing out a woman's inner beauty is the same as finding your inner voice. To me, Face Stockholm became a mission about healing, getting to one's inner truth, and ultimately about self-expression."

Martina decided that it was time to leave Manhattan, yet wanted to find a location that was still close by. She felt a strong connection to Upstate New York, and therefore established her office, distribution warehouse, and a branch store of Face Stockholm in nearby Hudson, New York. Soon, Martina found a house, and the move was complete. As she settled in, friends introduced her to David, a successful restaurateur (owner of Santa Fe in Tivoli, New York, and Max's Barbeque in Red Hook, New York), and some time later they were married. Little did David know that the house they would eventually live in was just a few feet south of the house he was currently living in.

Both Martina and David individually had admired the property over the years, and when it came up for sale, David didn't hesitate to buy it. According to Martina and David, the light that is

Martina Arfwidson, vice president of Face Stockholm, and her husband, restaurateur David Weiss, lovingly restored and added to their American turn-of-the-century farmhouse, creating an interior that is light-filled and Swedish-inspired. The idea was not only to restore the house but to transform a small antique farmhouse into a spacious, architecturally interesting farmhouse with an urban loft thrown in.

cast into the house during all daylight hours reminds them of the light cast into a greenhouse. The effect is what attracted them and inspired them to build a spacious addition that captured that light indoors. David began the restoration project. David's other business, Clay Hill, specializes in design restoration and architectural new construction design projects; therefore, this house was right up his alley. David's keen architectural and design eye and Martina's gifted design aesthetic transformed the late-nineteenth-century American farmhouse into a spacious, sun-filled home that has the warmth and essence of a greenhouse. You can't help but feel happy and energized when entering the house, and that is the effect that both Martina and David strived to accomplish.

Martina's natural Swedish approach to interiors lies in her choice of colors and accessories. Historically, Swedish interiors were based on capturing as much exterior light as possible, due to the lack of sunlight during the winter months. Crystal, mirrors, and lighter interior colors were used to reflect light into the house. Martina's design incorporates these principles, and while not typically Swedish in style, her home reflects the soul of Swedish style and elegance. ❈

Martina became familiar with the house while living near the property and spent plenty of time looking at the land there. What attracted her to the property was the magnificent river view and how the light entered the home. As fate would have it, David purchased the house a few years later.

OPPOSITE: Swedish antiques collected by Martina gracefully pepper the living room. The confidence to incorporate contemporary furniture with antique is truly Scandinavian.

THIS PAGE, TOP: Martina and David's kitchen is a culinary dream. Designed by David, the space is both a continuation of the mood set by the house as well as a professionally functional kitchen where space to create is abundant.

THIS PAGE, BOTTOM: Introducing color into the living room is achieved through the natural simplicity of hydrangeas and a late-summer pumpkin.

OPPOSITE, TOP: One of the elements that made the house so special to Martina and David was the greenhouse feeling inside. Inspired by this, Martina has scattered many different potted plants throughout the house so that you truly get the sense of being in a greenhouse.

OPPOSITE, BOTTOM: Streaming sunshine and a stunning river view transform a bedroom into a refuge from daily life.

THIS PAGE: Windows dominate the room, allowing nature to take over and capture the interior. The reading corner in the master bedroom is reminiscent of the summer pavilions in Sweden. The pavilion, during the late eighteenth and nineteenth centuries, served as an escape to read and reflect while surrounded by the beauty of nature.

THIS PAGE: The mirror is strategically placed to capture as much exterior light as possible, the windows lack any obstruction, and the interior colors are light and inviting. Though simple, the use of these three design elements creates a master bath that is sophisticated elegance.

OPPOSITE, TOP: The store interiors of Face Stockholm are inspired by the Swedish aesthetic. The product is merchandised for easy approachability, and the use of lighter interior colors allows for comfortable shopping and focus in creating the right color palette for each individual client; lighter interior colors allow for better interior lighting as light is reflected rather than absorbed as it would be with darker interior colors.

OPPOSITE, BOTTOM: Established in Sweden in 1980 by Martina's mother, Gun Nowak, Face Stockholm has become an international force in the world of cosmetics and is now co-owned and operated by Martina and Gun. Based in Sweden with U.S. operations in Upstate New York, Martina and Gun have retail stores in Sweden, Ireland, Norway, and the United States.

quiet confidence

PAUL AND SUSANNE SIGENLAUB RESIDENCE, NEW YORK

For over two decades, Evergreen has been a restful oasis from the kinetic energy of Manhattan's Third Avenue. Owned by antique dealer Paul Sigenlaub, the shop is known as a mainstay for designers and collectors seeking out fine Scandinavian and Baltic antiques. Upon entering the store, you are transported into an ethereal world of light dancing off crystal, gilding, and mirrors. With a quick glance around at the ormolu and marquetry commodes and gilt consoles topped by rare porphyry vases, you can see that you have entered a realm devoted to exploring the influential tastes of the Gustavian court.

OPPOSITE: Eames leather dining chairs with casters team up with an 1830s Swedish demilune dining table in faux bois d'arc. A traditional Swedish Christmas candelabra made of tin sits on the dining table. Against the dining room wall rests an East German cupboard with baroque blanket box holders in the shape of dogs.

THIS PAGE: This claw-footed Gustavian bench is signed by Johan Vogt.

Historically, the Gustavian style met with and was distilled into the roots of Swedish tradition when it traveled from the cities into the Swedish countryside. This country furniture, using simpler native materials and paints, yet keeping the elegant lines of its city counterparts, first appealed to Paul many years ago, when he was a dealer in Americana. "My wife, Susanne, is Danish, and we were living in Upstate New York with many of her family heirlooms. I had always loved Scandinavian antiques, but it was Susanne who really expanded my curiosity about them. What's always interested me is the abstraction of the naïve. These incredible folk pieces, or *allmoge* as they say in Swedish, with the crazy exaggerated paint . . . the abstract quality is the same as looking at a contemporary work of art."

The couple bought a late-nineteenth-century fisherman's house in Rungsted Kyst on the Danish coast just twenty minutes north of Copenhagen with a view of Skåne, Sweden, across the sound. Susanne lovingly tended the eighteenth-century garden at the house and filled it with a collection of Scandinavian garden furniture. It was there, while living in the town that Karin Blixen made famous, that the couple was able to fully immerse themselves in their passion for Scandinavian furniture.

Paul and Susanne's New York apartment, though small and not initially appealing, was in the heart of Manhattan, had a sizable terrace, and was filled for most of the day with plenty of natural sunlight. Recognizing an opportunity, the couple began renovations and eventually merged two adjoining apartments together. The renovations entailed removing walls and stripping some of the old interior. Intent on

THIS PAGE: A gilt Gustavian mirror above an early-nineteenth-century country Swedish demilune table suggests the wonderful pairings of formal and primitive to be discovered within Paul and Susanne's home.

OPPOSITE: Danish designer Kaare Klint's 1930s leather chairs make a striking contrast to a 1790 Klismos settee attributed to Stockholm chair maker Ephraim Ståhl.

creating a blank canvas, the walls were painted a diluted limestone and the flooring was given a white lime finish in the traditional Swedish manner. Simple window treatments, gallery lighting, and an elegant method of concealing the radiators finished off the space. What resulted is a cool, sleek backdrop for Paul and Susanne's collection—a felicitous mixture of modern and antique Scandinavian furniture and powerful American contemporary art.

"It is just things we have come to live with," says Paul. The treasures on display run the gamut from an Arne Jacobsen "Egg Chair" to a rare collection of large Scandinavian wood-carved folk art horses.

What all of the objects have in common is Paul's discerning eye and passion for quality design. "I am not so much concerned in my own home with provenance as I am with the integrity and form of a piece. An old, handcrafted farmer's candle stand from the Swedish countryside is just as beautiful to me as a formal table made by a Stockholm cabinetmaker. The interest for me lies in the strength of the form," says the antiques dealer. "There is a strong connection and almost a dialog between these Swedish eighteenth- and nineteenth-century pieces and the twentieth-century Scandinavian modern furniture here in the apartment. They mix together well." ❁

LEFT: An Ephraim Ståhl 1780 Swedish armchair, upholstered in leather, sits in front of a large oil painting by Danish painter Henry Heerup, a member of the European postwar CoBrA movement. The painting was purchased from the artist by Susanne's father, a noted journalist and art critic.

RIGHT: The strong lines on an early-nineteenth-century, blue-painted Swedish chest of drawers are juxtaposed with the lines of the primary-colored wall sculpture by American artist Donald Judd.

A traditional early-nineteenth-century
Swedish secretary in faux bois d'arc-and-
blue adds character to the bedroom. It is
topped by a ceremonial Swedish wedding
distaff from the early 1800s.

OPPOSITE: An Arne Jacobsen "Egg Chair" sits between a nineteenth-century Swedish white-painted candle stand and a miniature trestle table topped in glass. A work by Joel Shapiro is the central focus of the den.

THIS PAGE, TOP: An eighteenth-century Swedish cupboard was painted in an exuberant blue-and-white pattern meant to mimic marble.

THIS PAGE, BOTTOM: A precious nineteenth-century Swedish tobacco box made of birch bark was painted to simulate marble.

STORE HOURS
Monday – Saturday
10 am – 5 pm
Sunday 12 pm – 5 pm

Available by private appointment
203-263-7030

Entrance

1760 thompson house

ELEISH VAN BREEMS ANTIQUES, WOODBURY, CONNECTICUT

When Edie and I were establishing our business in 1997, we began by looking for the right location. While living in Woodbury ("the Antiques Capital of Connecticut") and traveling down Main Street on an errand, I noticed a "for sale" sign in front of the Nationally Registered 1760 Thompson House. Aware that historic houses do not stay on the market for long, I quickly hurried home to call Edie. The following day, we toured Thompson House and decided that this property would be the perfect spot for our antiques business.

OPPOSITE: Built in 1760 by Hezekiah Thompson, Esq., the first lawyer and magistrate of Woodbury, Connecticut, the Thompson House was considered a mansion in its time. The prior owners, Ransom and Rosemary Wright, lovingly restored the property after it had fallen under years of neglect, and, ironically, they chose to paint the house Falun red with white trim, the color of most Swedish farmhouses.

THIS PAGE: A late-eighteenth-century Swedish settee, gilt Rococo mirror, and Dutch seventeenth-century garden sculpture of Hercules by Matthieu von Beveran (Antwerp 1630–80), simply placed, define Swedish elegance. The lack of window treatments and floor coverings enhances the feeling of simplicity as well as allows for light to stream in unobstructed. Originally darker, the pine flooring was stripped, bleached, and pickled to add authenticity to the Swedish Gustavian parlor. In the seventeenth, eighteenth, and nineteenth centuries, the pine floors were cleaned and treated with water and sand, creating that wonderfully distressed flooring; however, it is much easier in modern times to bleach and pickle.

Now that the location was determined, Edie and I headed off to Europe to find our new treasures. Uninspired by what we came across, we decided to focus on Swedish antiques while on the tarmac in Sweden during a stopover that was meant only to visit family. Given that my great-aunt, Ingvor Gullers, had been a well-known dealer in Sweden, the path was perhaps an easier one than for most. Mormor, as she is known, helped us tremendously with her connections and wisdom, as well as did my aunt Ittan Gullers.

When Edie and I returned to the United States, Edie's mother, Diane Ekholm Valente (Swedish on her father's side) was thrilled to discover that we had defined the focus for our store as Swedish. Edie and I like to say that the decision to focus on Swedish antiques and reproduction furniture was more an act of divine intervention than of anything contrived.

As we anxiously awaited the arrival of our first container, we prepared the house by painting the interior with hand-mixed pigment paints imported from Sweden and by bleaching and then pickling the pine floorboards.

Pickling is done simply by bringing the wood down to its raw state and then applying white pickling stain (which can be found at any paint store). Once the stain has been applied, the next step is to wipe the area down with a soft cloth (an old T-shirt is ideal), leaving only a hint of color. This process creates an effect that is similar to the look of antique Swedish flooring. After the stain is wiped off sufficiently and the wood has dried, you can layer a few coats of clear polyurethane to seal it. This process takes a good twenty-four hours or more to dry and cure. Climates also vary; in more humid

THIS PAGE: Due to the very long winter months when sunlight is a luxury, Swedish interiors have had to adapt to the darkness, and as a result, lighter, less-structured colors have become the base for Swedish design. The practical approach to creating a lighter, happier space has resulted in the birth of simple elegance. A period seventeenth-century Rococo armoire, a pair of eighteenth-century Gustavian side chairs, early-twentieth-century Gustavian-style crystal sconces, and a mid-twentieth-century Swedish rag runner complete the room.

OPPOSITE: We wanted to lend authenticity to the eighteenth-century Swedish parlor and, therefore, decided to use Swedish pigment paints, imported from Sweden. The paints were hand-mixed using mineral spirits, Swedish pigments, boiled linseed oil, and a dryer, and we spent countless hours layering the paint in the front parlor of the house. According to Edie, "In order to truly capture the essence of refracted light cast off the painted interior walls found in period manor homes in Sweden, we felt that it was essential to re-create the process they had used centuries before us." Though it was very time-consuming, waiting for each layer to dry before applying the next, we found that over the years clients responded to the pigmented walls instinctively, acknowledging their authenticity and point of difference.

environments, this process takes much longer.

We felt that it was essential to re-create the wonderful paint surfaces that the antique homes in Sweden have (as well as the blonde flooring) in order to create a lifestyle antiques shop that felt more like a private residence than a business. The challenge was to implement an authentic Swedish interior in a National Historic Registered American home so that each person who entered through the front door felt a natural transition from eighteenth-century America to eighteenth-century Sweden. To our surprise, that transition was easier to achieve than we thought.

The next step in the Thompson House transformation was to convert what had been a traditionally formal Williamsburg-inspired garden, established by the previous owners, Ransom and Rosemary Wright, into a natural Swedish garden more akin to an English sensibility. Edie, an avid gardener, had a long-term vision of what the garden should look like and began the journey with great enthusiasm. With a great connection to the garden, both emotionally and technically, Edie achieved her vision but, as with all projects, still continues to alter and tweak it as the years pass. The garden has truly enhanced the experience, and, as in Sweden, the connection with the interior and exterior fall hand in hand. ❁

Imagine the writing room of a seventeenth-century Swedish noble. Feather quills are displayed for writing letters, a birch-bark tobacco canister sits next to a small barrel flask reserved for vodka, an iron candleholder is poised for use, and a favored companion sits faithfully waiting for his master's acknowledgment. Reflective of the nobility's education, a leather-bound Bible awaits reference, and engravings (*Suecia Antiqua et Hodierna or Ancient and Modern Sweden*, published 1660–1716) by Count Erik Jönsson Dahlberg (1625–1703), the famous Swedish engineer, hang simply on the wall. The luxury of heat is provided by the ceramic stove in the corner.

While the gray-white Swedish Gustavian style has captivated the marketplace for the last ten years or so, little is written about the colorful and robust Swedish country folk furniture, otherwise known as *allmoge*. Many of the forms applied in *allmoge* furniture were derived from the noble furniture; however, due to cost and availability of materials, the end results were a more dressed-down version. Colors applied to these pieces were determined by the availability of certain pigments. Yellow came from yellow ochre, blue from the indigo plant, red from copper ore, black from iron ore, white from zinc oxide, and brown from the earth. This nineteenth-century bed settee is a wonderful example of an *allmoge* piece that is Gustavian in form, yet country in style. Simpler than a nobleman's settee would be, this country piece is still carved and detailed, making it beautiful in its own right.

THIS PAGE, TOP: Midsummer in Sweden is a time for celebration. Sunlight is abundant, and the mood is festive. The Saturday between June 20 and 26 is a national holiday in Sweden—an old pagan celebration dating back to the Vikings. Midsummer marks the longest day of summer (summer solstice) and was originally a fertility rite where the maypole, a phallic representation, symbolically impregnated Mother Nature. The result of this ritual was in hopes of a bountiful harvest come fall. Traditional fare for a mid-summer party is plenty of herring, potatoes, and lots of ice-cold aquavit, beer, and snaps. Also less traditional, yet still plentiful, are crayfish, fruit, cheese, and vodka. A mid-summer gathering is a special time to reconnect with family and friends.

THIS PAGE, BOTTOM: A close-up of our Swedish garden in bloom. The garden has flourished over the years, and we are constantly at work adding plantings that complement what we inherited from Rosemary Wright, the previous owner. We continue to expand the garden to fit our vision of a traditional Swedish country garden.

OPPOSITE: The upstairs guest bedroom is the perfect example of how Swedish reproduction furniture mixes very well with Swedish period antiques. Incorporating items from the Eleish van Breems reproduction line, such as this Gustavian-style bed, small oval mirror, and the two Gustavian-style chairs, with a nineteenth-century Gustavian-style commode and small writing table, allows the collector freedom to find items that might be otherwise difficult to come by as an antique.

scandinavian modern

HOME OF RESTAURANT AQUAVIT'S HÅKAN AND CATHERINE SWAHN

As one of New York's premier restaurateurs, Håkan Swahn has long dazzled Americans with haute, modern Swedish cuisine at his innovative restaurant Aquavit. His taste for all things modern and Scandinavian may also be found in the well-appointed aerie, nestled above Central Park, that he has created for himself and his wife, Catherine, and their young son, Niclas. Though filled with a fine collection of furniture by modern masters, the Swahn home is neither stringent nor formal. It is a light-drenched series of open rooms and, like Aquavit, a welcoming place of ease in the heart of the city.

OPPOSITE: The Poul Kjaerholm chair is the perfect example of the mid-twentieth-century modern Scandinavian aesthetic—natural materials of wood, leather, and metal, gracefully combined.

THIS PAGE: Håkan's signature brand of aquavit sits on a teak tray with a pepper grinder.

The aesthetic of Scandinavian modernism is
something that Håkan was exposed to from an early
age. His father was, for a time, a successful Swedish
antiques dealer, so Håkan was lucky to be acquainted
with the best in Swedish traditional furniture. "Dad
was really, really into collecting the *allmoge*," says
Håkan, referring to the folk furniture of Sweden.
"When you have someone that close to you with that
much knowledge it just rubs off a little." It was one of
his best friend's homes, however, that would have a
lasting effect on him. "My friend's father was an architect and had some of the best examples of Swedish
and Danish modernism that had just been produced.
They had the most amazing collection. Designers like
Hans Wegner, Bruno Mathsson, Piet Hein. Of

course, I didn't know who they were at the time—I
just knew that I really, really liked this furniture! Now
I am a collector."

Håkan's furniture is complemented by art from
both Swedish and New York artists. He loves to buy
at auction and has recently been consumed in putting
together a delightful collection of teak ice buckets and
peppermills by Danish designer Jens Quistgaard to
grace the tables of his home and Aquavit. In fact, most
of the interior of the restaurant is echoed in Håkan's
living space, and you begin to understand how intri-
cately Håkan's tastes and interests are the driving
vision for Aquavit.

Architect Michel Franck was brought in by
Håkan and Catherine to convert the cramped rooms

of their apartment into a more open layout. "It was very important that we have a large open area to entertain. I come from a very large family, and we love to gather here with all of the children," says Catherine. "We put in the Italian sliding doors so that we can easily close off that area of the living room and use it as a guest bedroom and Niclas's playroom. I love that by taking down the traditional standing walls the rooms have become more versatile."

When Aquavit's lease was up, Franck and Swahn took the stylish Nordic concept of the Swahn's apartment and incorporated it into the new location and decor of the restaurant. Located on the ground floor of an office tower on Fifty-Fifth Street, the restaurant boasts a large 12,000-square-foot space. Franck and Swahn took advantage of the space and created dramatic features such as a soaring and undulating ash ceiling, giant circular recessed lighting, and walls of glass, oak, and slate—all of which serve to showcase the Scandinavian modern furnishings throughout the dining rooms. The restaurant's interior is rich with surprising and wonderful uses of natural materials. "Very Scandinavian," says Håkan of the restaurant's interior. It's the perfect backdrop for Aquavit's surprising and wonderful Scandinavian cuisine. ✽

THIS PAGE: Sculptural ice buckets and pepper-mills by Jens Quistgaard for Dansk. Håkan loves to buy at auction and has recently been consumed in putting together a delightful collection of these items.

OPPOSITE: A comfortable seating area is arranged around the Hans Wegner coffee table in the den. The Swedish armchair was salvaged from being burnt by Håkan's father during a tuberculosis epidemic in 1920s Sweden. At that time in Sweden it was still thought by some that all personal effects of an individual who contracted tuberculosis could potentially be contagious and therefore must be destroyed. Reupholstered in butter-cream yellow, the chair is now a prized possession.

OPPOSITE: Sliding glass and wood doors lend versatility and drama to the apartment floor plan.

THIS PAGE: Works by Swedish artist Peter Dahl hang in the master bedroom. The lamps by Luxus are from Håkan's childhood home. A green-and-white Klippan Swedish blanket adds a warming touch.

THIS PAGE: The sleek dining room, furnished in twentieth-century Scandinavian modern, transports the diner to Nordic realms.

OPPOSITE: In the dramatic bar at Aquavit, Swedish hospitality is teamed with Scandinavian contemporary designs. Clear glass containers of flavored aquavits line the walls of the lounge and are ready for sampling.

swedish inspiration

JOANN BARWICK'S FLORIDIAN ESCAPE AND VERMONT STUDIO

JoAnn Barwick has been on the cutting edge of Scandinavian style during her long career in publishing. Editor-in-chief of *House Beautiful* magazine for more than a decade, as well as the founding editor of *Country Living* magazine, JoAnn truly fell in love with the elegance and simplicity of Scandinavian design. In 1991, after visiting so many beautiful locations throughout Norway (the homeland of both sets of her grandparents), Sweden, Finland, and Denmark, JoAnn decided that the natural thing for her to do was to publish a book on the Scandinavia she encountered. As a result, *Scandinavian Country*, published by Clarkson Potter, was soon out on the market and in everyone's coffee table collection. JoAnn's vision made her a pioneer, and since leaving the publishing world, she has designed numerous collections for major furniture manufacturers, including a Swedish Gustavian-inspired line, thus continuing her influence in the market.

OPPOSITE: This Gustavian faux *kakelugn* cabinet is one of JoAnn's favorite pieces from her line of Swedish furniture that she designed, in collaboration with Martine Colliander, for "Solgarden." Frequently in the grand manor homes of Sweden, where symmetry was essential, the formal parlors would have an impressive ceramic stove cabinet that was an exact visual match in the opposite corner.

THIS PAGE: Island life is the perfect setting for Swedish style. The essence of why summers in Sweden are so prized is that they allow people to open up their house to nature, letting the sun saturate the interior.

JoAnn and her husband, Fred Berger, spend the summer and fall in Vermont and then venture down to the west coast of Florida in the winter and spring. The Vermont home is everything that the best of New England has to offer. Beautiful rolling hills and scenic views complement the property, making JoAnn's base studio a dream to create in. In designing the addition that would become her studio, JoAnn looked towards a traditional Swedish pavilion, or *lusthuset*, for inspiration. In essence, the idea was to create a space that was inviting and filled with light. Historically, the long dark winters of Sweden made the Swedes cherish sunlight, and as a result, summer pavilions were an essential part of summer life.

In concert with the structural theme, JoAnn chose a Swedish palette for her studio to enhance the mood of the space. Faux finishing the floors in the style of Skogaholm Manor at Skansen and applying white as a base with shades of blue to highlight, she created a crisp, elegant, and light-filled environment for her creativity to run free.

Located on the west coast of Florida, JoAnn and Fred's second home can be described as a New England–style home. The interior is sunny and welcoming due to the spacious layout, abundance of windows, and soft Swedish colors. In designing the house, JoAnn also wanted to capture the beauty of the location, and therefore

included an attached gazebo, or pavilion, where she, Fred, and their family could enjoy the outdoors.

The floor plan of the dining room was increased to accommodate the Swedish Gustavian-inspired dining room furniture "Solgarden" created in collaboration with JoAnn and Martine Colliander. Peppered throughout the house are additional items from the "Solgarden" collection, including a wonderfully painted faux *kakelugn* cabinet derived from the Swedish sense of symmetry. Historically found in the manor homes of the late eighteenth and nineteenth centuries, the *kakelugn*, or ceramic stove, was installed in larger rooms as well as bedrooms and provided a great source of warmth. To accommodate the Swedish sense of interior balance, a faux *kakelugn* replica was placed on the matching side of the room to visually balance the actual working stove. These cabinets also served a functional purpose in providing additional storage, so not only was there a visual application but a practical one as well.

Currently, JoAnn is designing for Drexel Heritage as well as a new line of Scandinavian lighting fixtures for the Frederick Cooper Company called "Nordic Lights." JoAnn's vision and perfectionist eye continue to be an inspiration to us all as she constantly reaches for new and interesting design ideas. ❖

THIS PAGE: Blue-and-white antique *faïence* chargers displayed on the wall are part of JoAnn's extensive collection.

OPPOSITE: JoAnn's collection of seashells add a Floridian touch to the otherwise Swedish-inspired interior.

THIS PAGE: A pair of wonderful rush-backed barrel armchairs, designed by JoAnn, add a tropical touch to the Swedish-inspired furniture, which was designed by JoAnn as well.

OPPOSITE: Blue-and-white antique Canton ware—part of JoAnn's extensive collection of antique French, English, Dutch, and Asian blue-and-white *faience*—are cleverly displayed, continuing the blue-and-white theme throughout the house.

OPPOSITE: This light and airy dining room inspired by the Swedish Gustavian period lends itself as a wonderful space for JoAnn and her husband, Fred, when hosting dinner parties for family and friends. As with a majority of the furniture in the house, the dining table and chairs were designed by JoAnn and Martine Collinder, in collaboration with Solgarden.

THIS PAGE: Shades of blue, in both classical and contemporary pieces, work together to create a balanced space.

OPPOSITE: The blue-and-white color scheme throughout the house ties all the rooms together and tells a very strong design story. Touches of French toile add to the creative approach that JoAnn has taken. During the Gustavian period, toile from France would have been imported and found in the finer homes of Stockholm and Gothenburg; therefore, JoAnn's use of toile is not only beautiful, it is also historically accurate.

THIS PAGE, TOP: Samples from Swedish chair makers that she has collected during her trips to Sweden provide a glimpse into JoAnn's sensibilities as a designer of furniture and accessories.

THIS PAGE, BOTTOM: Blue-and-white Scottish antique carpet balls add a touch of whimsy.

Displayed with JoAnn's collection of
faience is a wonderful example of a
nineteenth-century Swedish armoire,
a gift from her husband, Fred.

Traditionally, in the finer homes of Sweden, it was not uncommon to find a small summer pavilion or gazebo hiding somewhere on the property. The pavilion was used during the warm summer months for reflection, flirting, or an intimate tea party. In keeping with this tradition, JoAnn and Fred can enjoy those moments in their attached pavilion that overlooks a tranquil, private pond.

THIS PAGE: Imagine sitting on the front terrace on a warm summer night enjoying your family and surrounding garden.

OPPOSITE: JoAnn's Vermont studio was inspired by a traditional Swedish pavilion, or *lusthuset*. She designed a space to create in that was sun-filled and in touch with nature. Incorporating a skylight into the design also allowed for more sunlight to be captured inside; it also gives the illusion that the earth and sky are one and all is in balance.

THIS PAGE: With much of the building open to the surrounding gardens via the abundance of windows, JoAnn chose an interior color palette that would enhance the space and attract light. The introduction of color is limited to a few accessories, including the coffee table, which acts as an anchor for the room.

OPPOSITE: Inspired by the painted floors of Skogaholm Manor found at the outdoor museum, Skansen, in the city of Stockholm, JoAnn re-created the grid pattern in her Vermont studio. Not only does the pattern make the space seem grander in size, but the light-colored palette also allows for the sun to reflect onto yet another surface, producing more interior light.

stylish barn living
STEVE AND KATIE HYLÉN'S RESIDENCE, CONNECTICUT

Nestled into a rolling hillside in Litchfield County, a traditional dairy barn stood until Steve and Katie Hylén converted it into a stunning modern home that unfolds seamlessly into nature. The couple, open-minded and adventuresome by nature, came unexpectedly upon the white barn while on a drive. The door had been left open and the place appeared to be abandoned. Walking into the massive 15,000-square-foot barn, Steve quickly became excited about the possibilities and challenges of converting the barn into a home. "I was not looking for a dairy barn in particular!" says Steve laughing, "I was looking for space—raw space. It wouldn't have mattered if it was an

OPPOSITE: The hearth was the single most important feature in the Swedish home. To this day, the hearth fire represents food, warmth, and a sustaining gathering spot. Steve and Katie made their hearth the focal point of their great room with ample seating for their many guests.

THIS PAGE: A view of the barn from the side entrance.

airplane hanger. What I was interested in was the potential of such a large area."

An award-winning commercial photographer and director turned inventor, Steve was undaunted by the size of the project and so the conversion began. After purchasing the property, the existing stalls, feed pipes, and troughs had to be removed, and the concrete flooring had to be lifted out to make way for a large radiant heating system. The flooring turned out to be four feet thick, but the Hyléns soldiered on, gaining a lower floor and vaulted ceilings. To add light, Steve and Katie made the dramatic decision to take down an entire side and corner of the barn and replace them with soaring glass windows held in place by steel girders. What results is a beauty of contrasts—the steel and glass set against the soft, rolling Litchfield hills.

In Sweden there is a word, *brukskonst*, which means "useful art." Function always comes before beauty. This respect for economy and intimacy with nature, as raw materials were extremely limited, is an integral part of Sweden's design psyche. Examples of *brukskonst* abound at the Hyléns' home. Steve learned forging from his grandfather, who was a master Swedish ironsmith, and throughout the house are won-

derful iron chandeliers and candelabras that Steve made. The central seating area and focal point of the living room is a circular built-in sofa set around a giant hearth and oven that also serves as a beautiful amorphous sculpture. The hallway doubles as a sculptural installation with undulating walls and an unexpected fountain pond. The couple salvaged or recycled materials wherever possible, such as the steel beams, which came from Connecticut's old Danbury Fair. The more than forty eyebeam supports that Steve made to support the steel beams exemplify the Swedish spirit in that they are utilitarian, soundly designed, yet works of art unto themselves.

An intimate relationship with nature was a large part of Steve and Katie's philosophy when designing the home. "Growing up in Sweden, you would play outside in a box you climbed into. You were cocooned from the elements and then you would stick your head out," exclaims Steve. "Winter was raging all around you, but you were safe in your box. That was my concept in opening up the side of the barn to the view." Katie adds, "We lived there during the renovation process, which truly let us live outdoors in the elements. It was so amazing. When storms would come up, you were enthralled by their power. We still are. Living here we are in tune with the elements." ❀

PREVIOUS SPREAD: Built into the side of a hill, the barn overlooks commanding views of the surrounding countryside.

THIS PAGE: An artist's wooden model of a horse provides a dramatic focal point to the den. Katie, an accomplished equestrian, keeps her horse on the property.

OPPOSITE: To break up the length of the central hall that runs almost half the length of the barn, Steve made the walls curve and undulate. In the center of the hall, a Zen rock pool with bubbling fountain is a peaceful happening.

OPPOSITE: Katie and Steve left the large expanse of tiled floor open around the hearth area, ensuring that its circular shape is viewed in a sculptural way. Light and shadows play all day on the tile floor.

THIS PAGE: In the dining area of the great room, the table is fit for a banquet. The candles are poised to be lit in candle stands forged and collected by Steve. Candlelight is a central part of Swedish life.

THIS PAGE: The fireplace, kitchen oven, and chimneystack are all designed as a single curving piece of sculpture. The amorphous quality is heightened by the straight lines of the structure around it.

OPPOSITE: The worktable doubles as a casual dining spot to watch the cook. Surfaces in the kitchen are clutter free, and cabinets have been eschewed for open windows. A large pantry closet with steel shelving hides the necessities.

studio in manhattan
THE GUSTAVIAN STUDIO OF LENA BIÖRCK KAPLAN

The charmed Manhattan studio of Lena Biörck Kaplan, owner of the Swedish design shop White on White, now Studio White on White, is not only a work space but also a pause point where she can escape the rush of everyday life. In 1995, Lena made a visit to the shop Solgarden, in Stockholm, where she met owner Martine Colliander, whom she calls her "inspiration, soul sister, and wonderful colleague." "After I saw Martine's shop, I was haunted by pictures of this grayish-white environment. It was very beautiful to me. There were only three rooms,

OPPOSITE: The confidence in mixing old with new is part of the Swedish design sensibility. Lena chose a reproduction Gustavian dining table and chairs as her functional pieces and then added a nineteenth-century Gustavian bed settee for flavor. In the nineteenth century, the Swedish bed settee served as a trundle bed at night and a settee during the day. It was not uncommon for several family members to sleep together in the same bed. This not only saved valued space but also kept everyone warm during the cold winter season. Today, the bed settee is still used as seating; however, the function has changed from a bed to a wonderful area for a little extra storage. With easy accessibility (the seat lifts up), the settee offers a perfect spot for toys, blankets, or linens.

THIS PAGE: Artist Charles Kivowitz's painting complements the design palette of Lena's studio.

candlelight, flowers, music—nobody there. And then, Martine came out. She had been painting. There was something about this concept that I could see would work for a busy city like New York."

Inspired by Solgarden, Lena, with the help of Martine, opened the doors to White on White in June 1999. It was a dream come true for Lena, and, after three years, she expanded and opened Studio White on White, offering some of White on White products to retailers nationally. "At Studio White on White, we show Gustavian furniture, accessorized with embroidered textiles, rugs, quilts, curtains, pillows, nightwear by White Sense, and ceramics." The White Sense line, exclusive to Studio White on White, was created because "what else could be united with the simplicity and purity of everyday life that White on White presents, than a clear white cotton line!"

Lena's success is due to her clients' interest in her design sensibility. Her large following has responded so well because "it's a look of simple beauty; there is harmony in it. These days, especially with all of the running around, it's great to have a little more quiet." The Studio White on White space is a direct reflection of that sensibility. After acquiring the studio space four years ago, Lena installed moldings, ragged the walls, pickled the floors, and hung billowing, sun-drenched linens designed by Martine, creating 1600 square feet of tranquility in the middle of bustling Midtown Manhattan.

For seven years, Lena owned and operated White on White but has since chosen to close the store and focus on Studio White on White. It will still carry all of the beautiful inventory that the retail store carried but in a studio environment instead. According to Lena, in regards to shop ownership, "We've had a wonderful time. The joys of working together on something creative—that is what really gives you joy in life." Lena is ready, excited, and poised for phase two. ❁

In keeping with the great manor homes and royal palaces of Sweden, decorative wall coverings on canvas, by muralist Jonas Wikman, add elegance and a neoclassical element to the studio.

THIS PAGE: A crisp, neutral palette reflects the color of earth and sky. As the sunlight streams in through the window, the Gustavian-style bed offers a welcoming resting spot for reflection.

OPPOSITE: Sunlight and nature account for much of Swedish interiors. By keeping the floors and walls light and having little or no window treatments, the sun can filter into the space and reflect off of the pale interior colors. Floral bouquets are kept very simple using mostly wild flowers, and tabletop arrangements boast fruits in season.

Lena relishes her time spent at the office. "I always had my eye on this building with the idea of making myself a completely luxurious office. It's not that I need it—it's that I deserve it!" she says with a mischievous grin. "It's not unusual for me to be here on Sundays."

acknowledgments
RHONDA ELEISH

First and foremost, I would like to thank Jon Monson and my husband, L. L Ergmann ("Buffer") of Endo Graphics, Danbury, Connecticut, for their beautiful images. This book is truly the result of wonderful collaboration between four people. Jon and Buffer's talent, vision, and stamina truly inspired Edie and me.

A very special thank-you to Albert Hadley for your generosity and support of this project. Thank you, thank you! We are truly honored!

A very special thank-you to Miguel Flores-Vianna for your vision and love of Swedish design and interiors and for supporting that vision in your publications.

Thank you to my parents, Cathy and G. Eleish. Dad, your brilliant, artistic mind trained my eye at a young age; and Mom, your strength and loving support gave me balance. I love you!

Thank you and love to Francis Causbie, my grandmother. I wish you were here to help proofread!

Thank you to my new daughter, Kari Eleish Ergmann, for a wonderful pregnancy while producing this book and tremendous joy while editing. Your coos and smiles have kept me going. I love you!

Thank you also to my family: my sister, P. Eleish and family, the Elliott family, the Dittus family, Sara Wills Anderson, David and Ariana Ganak, and Yola and Nick Mourginis.

To Patty Clark, our former general manager of Eleish van Breems Antiques, I thank you for putting up with us all these years. We will miss you, but celebrate your new venture with your husband, Chris . . . you go, girl!

Thank you to Jamie Arber for managing the store so well, allowing Edie and me to focus on this book.

Thank you to Cory Bowie and Mary Beth Keene for their friendship and support. Thank you to Jane Edwards for helping us with this project as well as connecting us to our agent, Linda Roghaar, of Linda Roghaar Literary Agency, Inc. To Linda Roghaar, thank you for your help and guidance in all things literary. Thank you to all the members of WADA (Woodbury Antiques Dealers Association: www.antiqueswoodbury.com) in Woodbury, Connecticut, for your support. Thank you to Tim Tareco for your friendship and unconditional love.

Thanks to Mitch and Jessica Austin, Joyce and Bill Hoffman, Shelly and Peter Miller, Tom at Metal Works, Amy and Charles Rudick, Ingrid and Rich Gordon, Kristin and Charlie Allen, Ann and Jim Rae, Anne and John Gobron, Diana Beattie, Peggy Anderson, Mary Muryn, and Ms. Pia Lindstrom.

Thank you to Gabrielle Boström for your beautiful murals.

Thank you to Melinda Monson for taking such wonderful care of Tigger countless times while we were on the road. Thank you

OPPOSITE: A Gripsholm chair and ottoman are nestled into a snug corner by the tile stove. Hanging above the armchair is a corner cornice holding a dala horse from Loran Nordgren's collection.

to Pedro Guerra, our workshop manager and faux finisher, for your talent and dedication to your craft. Thanks to the team at Country Swedish for all of your help and support; to Lois and Jason Robards for always being so supportive no matter how hair-brained; to Julia Webber for letting us crash on your sofa countless times in Fulham. Thank you to Elisabeth Halvarsson-Stapen from The Consulate General of Sweden in New York for your amazing support and guidance with this project, and finally, to Mrs. Bergman, whose house always had the wonderful smell of Swedish cookies baking in the kitchen and whom I adored.

A very special thank you to my great-aunt Ingvor "Mormor" Gullers and my aunt Ittan Gullers, who were with us from the beginning and helped us navigate the antiques world in Sweden.

Thank you to my great-uncle, the photographer K. W. Gullers, whose powerful images of Sweden were imbedded in my mind from early childhood.

Thank you and love to my cousins Karin, Suzanne, Meg, Alexa, and Sergio.

Thank you to our Swedish mentor, Göte Järnefolk, for teaching us so much. Your knowledge and experience that you have so lovingly shared with us is—and will always be—invaluable.

A very special thank-you to our wonderful and very talented editor, Jennifer Grillone, to Suzanne Taylor for your vision, and to the wonderful team at Gibbs Smith, Publisher.

Thank you to Lucille Lortel for teaching me so many different things and being a huge influence in my life and to author and producer Vincent Curcio. My summers at The White Barn Theater changed my life!

To the team at Country Road Australia whom I grew up with . . . Thank you Danya for teaching me to believe in myself and thank you to Steve, Diedra, Tanya, Fred, David, Hillary, Stephanie, Lisa, Jay, Debbie, Bubba, Timmy, Jane and Meridith for a fun seven years!

Thank you to Greens Farms Academy, Greens Farms, Connecticut, and Sarah Lawrence College, Bronxville, New York.

To my partner in business and friendship, Edie, (or shall I say Oscar to my Felix?): thank you for your support and vision as we travel down this path together. Life would just not be as fun without you! Thank you for believing in me since the sixth grade!

And finally, thank you to all of the people who said "yes" to this project and allowed us to invade their homes and businesses to complete this book. Your talent and graciousness blew us away! ❁